JANUA LINGUARUM

STUDIA MEMORIAE
NICOLAI VAN WIJK DEDICATA

edenda curat

C. H. VAN SCHOONEVELD

Indiana University

Series Practica, 143

THE SYNTAX
OF THE SIMPLE SENTENCE
IN PROTO-GERMANIC

by

PAUL J. HOPPER

State University of New York, Binghamton

1975

MOUTON

THE HAGUE · PARIS

LIBRARY OF CONGRESS CATALOG CARD NUMBER: 72-94524

Printed in Belgium by NICI, Printers, Ghent

To Helen

PREFACE

This monograph is a modified version of a doctoral dissertation which was completed in 1967. Although the methodology and parts of the presentation have been somewhat changed, I have found no reason to alter the basic conclusions which I reached at that time, so that although quite naturally after a space of four years one would wish to undertake a complete revision of the work, I have in fact only made those alterations as would not interfere fundamentally with the format of the original work. It is my hope that the conclusions made will contribute a little toward our understanding of the elusive problem of Germanic sentence structure, and that the descriptive parts of the work can be used as a basis for further investigations. In both respects, of course, the work can at most claim to be preliminary and programmatic.

I wish to acknowledge with deep gratitude the many individuals and institutions who have made the completion of this monograph possible: Dr. Wayne Tosh and the staff of the University of Texas Linguistics Research Center, whose cooperation in the production of a computer-generated concordance to the Parker Manuscript helped provide an invaluable research tool; the committee who supervised the original dissertation: Professors Winfred P. Lehmann, Edgar C. Polomé, Robert D. King and Amar D. Singh; the University of Texas at Austin and Washington University, both of which have consistently provided stimulating academic environments conducive to scholarship; and other friends and colleagues too numerous to mention here, whose interests and abilities have been a constant challenge.

My debt in particular to Winfred P. Lehmann, both during my years as a student at the University of Texas and in the subsequent years during which he has maintained a close interest in my work and career, is one which cannot be repaid. His example as a scholar of stature who has nonetheless never ceased to inquire and to grow intellectually will be with me always.

Paul J. Hopper
St. Louis, 1971

CONTENTS

I

INTRODUCTION

A. STATEMENT OF THE PROBLEM

An interest in reconstructing syntactic, as well as phonological and morphological, patterns of the Germanic and Indo-European proto-languages is not a particularly new idea. Communalities in the syntax of the Germanic dialects are pointed out by Jacob Grimm in the *Deutsche Grammatik*, for example, and the period around the turn of the century saw the production of a number of works in book and article form concerning the question of 'word order' (*Wortstellung*), more properly surface constituent order.

In recent years, comparativists have again turned their attention to syntax, generally with a view to recovering abstract syntactic rules. Paul Kiparsky's article "Tense and Mood in Indo-European Syntax"[1] is likely to be a classic in both method and data for years to come, and Robin Lakoff's monograph *Abstract Syntax and Latin Complementation*[2] not only makes important general theoretical points, but indicates further kinds of data which students of comparative syntax can profitably work with. The implications of these and other recent works are that the preoccupation with surface word order, the position of the verb, the placing of enclitics, and so on, which characterized the work of the first decades of the twentieth century in this area, is in fact relatively trivial, since the rules which govern these aspects of syntax are late-level adjustment rules, and hence might be more susceptible of dialectal and individual variation. Furthermore, the diachronic changes in syntactic patterns are more satisfactorily accounted for by an investigation of the deeper constant structures from which the point of divergence between later stages of the language can be stated.

However, rather than attempting at this stage the production of the long series of formal grammars of early dialects which would be necessary for such an ideal account, I present in this monograph a discussion of some of the striking similarities between

---

[1] Paul Kiparsky, "Tense and Mood in Indo-European Syntax", *Foundations of Language* 4 (1968), 1:30-57.
[2] Robin Lakoff, *Abstract Syntax and Latin Complementation* (= *M.I.T. Research Monograph* No. 49) (Cambridge, M.I.T. Press, 1968).

the surface syntactic patterning of the early Germanic languages, and attempt on the basis of the parallels to relate Germanic and Indo-European sentence structures. It is not intended that this investigation be anything more than preliminary. It would perhaps even be an over-estimation to call it programmatic. Yet if the series of correspondences pointed to here are genuine correspondences, as they appear to be, they represent aspects of comparative Germanic linguistics, and perhaps of Indo-European linguistics, which ought to be susceptible of analysis in terms of a theory of language dealing with underlying, rather than purely surface, structures. The very durability of some of the 'surface' patterns which are discussed is perhaps itself a phenomenon which must be accounted for.

A further aspect of work with surface constituent ordering which must be taken into account is that of the typological implications following from Greenberg's investigations of word-order types.[3] From the kind of presentation made in this monograph a typological picture of Germanic and Proto-Indo-European may emerge. A few observations on Germanic and Indo-European sentence structure from this point of view will be made.[4]

B. SKETCH OF EARLIER RESEARCH

Fourquet, whose analysis[5] of the syntax of the early Germanic languages was intended to be based closely on a synchronic analysis of the individual dialects, with almost no concern for diachronic changes, sums up his discussion of Gothic with the statement that "From the point of view of positional syntax, Gothic belongs to the comparative study of the Indo-European languages rather than to the study of the Germanic languages."[6] He goes on to deplore the fact that the study of Indo-European syntax is so little advanced.[7] Fourquet, I believe, was aware that with his work scholarship had reached an impasse. It was possible to describe the syntactic features of any of the extant Germanic dialects, but not to combine such a description into a statement about Proto-Germanic syntax, even less to relate the Germanic features to Indo-European syntax. (Fourquet, who tried to draw some general conclusions from his synchronic studies of Germanic dialects, admitted that these conclusions could only be tentative.[8]) Any advance in the study of Germanic syntax could not come simply

---

[3] Joseph Greenberg, ed., *Universals of Language*, 2nd ed. (Cambridge, M.I.T. Press, 1966), pp. 73-113.

[4] Cf. Winfred P. Lehmann, "On the Rise of SOV Patterns in New High German", *Grammatik Kybernetik Kommunikation Festschrift für Alfred Hoppe*, K. G. Schweisthal, ed. (Bonn, Dümmler, 1971) and Emmon Bach, "Is Amharic an SOV Language?", *Journal of Ethiopian Languages*, 1970, for discussion of the diachronic significance of Greenberg's work.

[5] Jean Fourquet, *L'ordre des éléments de la phrase en germanique ancien; études de syntaxe de position* (Strasbourg, 1938).

[6] Fourquet, *L'ordre*, p. 284. Quotations from other languages are translated into English throughout, by the author.

[7] Fourquet, *L'ordre*, p. 284.

[8] Fourquet, *L'ordre*, p. 285.

by extrapolation from the extant dialects, but would have to be made hand in hand with the study of Indo-European syntax.

It is from this point of view that I will discuss previous research into Germanic and Indo-European word-order. No matter how neglected, a topic in the field of Indo-European and Germanic linguistics is likely to have an extensive bibliography. Restricting attention to studies relevant to Proto-Indo-European and Germanic syntax, I have collected some two hundred items, and have no doubt missed many others. In this summary of earlier work I will be concerned with a few of the more important studies. I will deal with Germanic and Indo-European syntax separately.

1. *Germanic Syntax*

The main discussion of Germanic syntax has always centered around the position of the verb in the clause, and especially the possibility of a contrast in Proto-Germanic between a main and a subordinate clause. Thus Tomanetz[9] and Erdmann[10] held that the second position — second in the sense of Modern German grammar — was original, and that the verb had drifted into final position in subordinate clauses at a later date in the history of German. Wackernagel, whose views I will later discuss in more detail, believed that Proto-Indo-European already possessed the contrast between second position of the verb in main clauses and final position in subordinate clauses.[11] Ries[12] and Delbrück[13] supported Wackernagel's view.

Braune[14] expressed the view, against Wackernagel, that the word order in Proto-Germanic was "free". In a later section of this chapter I will discuss the notion of free word order in more detail, because the claim that Proto-Indo-European sentences had unrestricted variety of word patterning has been maintained by other scholars, such as Hirt and Meillet.

Wackernagel's article "Über ein Gesetz der indo-germanischen Wortstellung" is of fundamental significance for both Proto-Indo-European and Proto-Germanic syntax. It represents the first attempt to formalize a rule of positional syntax for Proto-Indo-European and also the first evidence for a syntactic equation between Proto-Indo-European and Germanic. Wackernagel established that certain unstressed pronouns and particles in the Indo-European dialects tended to be placed after the first autonomous word in the clause, that is, in the second position in the sentence. He further observed that, since the verb in Sanskrit was accented in subordinate clauses but unaccen-

---

[9]   K. Tomanetz, Review of John Ries, *Stellung von Subject und Prädicatsverbum im Heliand*, *Deutsche Literaturzeitung* II (1881). 8:275.
[10]   Oskar Erdmann, *Grundzüge der deutschen Syntax nach ihrer geschichtlichen Entwicklung*, 1ste Abt (Stuttgart, Cotta, 1886), Part I, 193 fn.
[11]   Jacob Wackernagel, "Über ein Gesetz der Indogermanischen Wortstellung", *IF* 1 (1892):427.
[12]   John Ries, e.g., *Die Wortstellung im Beowulf* (Halle, Niemeyer, 1907), pp. 315-18.
[13]   Berthold Delbrück, *Germanische Syntax II*: *Zur Stellung des Verbums* (Leipzig, Teubner, 1911), pp. 14-16.
[14]   Wilhelm Braune, "Zur lehre von der deutschen Wortstellung", in *Forschungen zur deutschen Philologie*: *Festschrift für R. Hildebrand* (Leipzig, 1894), p. 50.

ted in main clauses, the verb of the main clause must have been "enclitic" and therefore had the positional feature of occurring second in the sentence in Proto-Indo-European; in other words, "the German rule for the position of the verb was already valid in the proto-language."[15]

Wackernagel's conclusions were greeted somewhat sceptically at first. Delbrück, although he later changed his views, did not at once accept the possibility of the enclitic verb in Proto-Indo-European.[16] In 1907, however, Ries published a statistical analysis of *Beowulf* in order to discover the positional features of the verb and the light elements in Old English. He concluded that Wackernagel's Law operated in Old English to the extent that clauses tended to end with heavy elements in Old English, and that the preference for ending a clause with a heavy element "pushed" the verb towards the position of the particles. But he saw in the statistical tendency for the verb to be postponed in subordinate clauses not the operation of Wackernagel's Law, but a reflection of the greater number of subordinate clauses which contained predicate pronouns.[17] In his review of Ries' study of word-order in *Beowulf*, Delbrück admitted that Wackernagel's Law applied fully to Proto-Germanic, and was an inheritance from Proto-Indo-European.[18] But in order to account for the frequent position of the finite verb immediately after an initial pronoun in the Germanic languages, he assumed that in Proto-Germanic pronouns were accented;[19] since there is no other evidence for accented pronouns in any of the Germanic or other extant Indo-European dialects, Delbrück's assumption must be regarded as a pure conjecture necessary in order to posit Wackernagel's Law unmodified in Proto-Germanic.

In 1933, Hans Kuhn published an article entitled "Zur Wortstellung und -betonung im Altgermanischen", in which he examined Germanic alliterative verse, especially Skaldic poetry, in order to discover rules of position of unaccented elements. He isolated what he called *Satzpartikeln* — particles having the whole clause rather than one constituent as their domain — and formulated the "law of particles" (*das germanische Satzpartikelgesetz*): "The sentence particles stand in the anacrusis, in proclisis to the first or second stressed word in the clause."[20] These particles were not to be equated positionally with the Indo-European enclitic particles, but rather stood in a later developed PROclisis to FOLLOWING autonomous elements. Despite Fourquet's scathing criticism of Kuhn's principles,[21] and the fact that Kuhn separates the positional features of the Germanic particles from those of Proto-Indo-European particles, Kuhn's work makes it clear that there is a parallel in the syntax of the particles in the two proto-languages.

[15] Wackernagel, "Über ein Gesetz":427.
[16] Berthold Delbrück, *Vergleichende Syntax der indogermanischen Sprachen* (Strassburg, Trübner, 1893-1900), vol. III, p. 82.
[17] Ries, *Die Wortstellung*, pp. 273-317.
[18] Delbrück, Review of Ries, p. 71.
[19] Delbrück, Review of Ries, p. 73 and *Syntax II*, p. 15.
[20] Hans Kuhn, "Zur Wortstellungen und -betonung im Altgermanischen", *PBB* 57 (1933):8.
[21] Cf. Fourquet, *L'ordre*, pp. 180-81.

The next work concerning Germanic syntax which I will discuss here is Fourquet's *L'ordre des éléments de la phrase en germanique ancien*. I have already suggested that Fourquet's study suffers from scepticism about the possibility of reconstructing syntagmatic features of Proto-Indo-European. Yet although Fourquet does not attempt to trace the development of syntagmatic features, he posits a number of stages, each represented by one of the dialects which he discusses. The first stage, represented by Gothic, has a neutral order noun-verb, and a MARKED[22] order verb-noun; the pronouns, however, have no important positional features, but appear before or after the verb, usually after it. At this stage there existed a number of elements which were not sufficiently autonomous (*suffisamment autonomes*) to appear at the head of the clause; these were the enclitics and certain other particles. The second stage, that of *Beowulf*, has light elements clustered at the beginning of the clause, with the verb preceding or following a noun; here the marked position of the verb is the sentence-initial one, and the neutral order has the verb in any position except the first. The third stage, that of the *Anglo-Saxon Chronicle* up to the year 892 A.D., and of the *Heliand*, has given up the contrast verb-noun/noun-verb and has either noun-verb alone, or else nouns "balanced" on either side of the verb. The light elements (particles and pronouns) remain before the verb, but are not so clearly at the head of the clause, and are better described as immediately preceding the verb. In the fourth stage, that of the remainder of the *Chronicle*, of *Isidor* and the *Edda*, the neutral sentence is characterized by either the second position of the verb, or another, "ulterior" position of the verb. "The difference between verb-second clause and ulterior-verb clause is here superimposed upon the *grammatical* difference between main and subordinate clause."[23]

Each one of these stages is presumably a reflex of a Proto-Germanic syntactic state, and in this respect Fourquet's analysis is relevant. But the dialects he discusses diverge not only chronologically, but also culturally and geographically; it is therefore difficult to accept them unconditionally as successive diachronic stages. In that he makes no attempt to reconstruct the syntactic patterns of Proto-Germanic, Fourquet's study does not cover the same ground as the present work, and has been only partially useful.

Karl Schneider's *Die Stellungstypen des finiten Verbs im urgermanischen Haupt- und Nebensatz*[24] represents an attempt to apply rough statistical methods to a number of corpora from several Germanic dialects. His method is praiseworthy, in that he draws on comparative Indo-European evidence and strives to derive Germanic and Proto-Germanic sentence-types from Proto-Indo-European sentence-types, and in that he does not place complete reliance on the exact statistical method. Schneider's

---

[22]   The term is not used by Fourquet. In the present study 'marked' refers to a word order which is not neutral or "habitual", but which deviates from the neutral order for a special effect. It is equivalent to Delbrück's *okkasionell* word-order, cf. Delbrück, *Vergleichende Syntax*, vol. III, p. 38.

[23]   Fourquet, *L'ordre*, p. 291.

[24]   (= *Untersuchungen und Texte* 41) (Heidelberg, Winter 1938).

effort is marred somewhat by his desire, for ideological reasons, to prove that the Germanic languages, because of a supposed freedom from adulterating non-Indo-European substrata, have preserved an original Proto-Indo-European word-order which in Indic succumbed to Dravidian, and in Latin to Etruscan influence. He assumes the initial position of the verb in the clause to be original in both Proto-Indo-European and Proto-Germanic, and admits an alternative sentence-type with final verb. To these he adds the possibility of a second position (but not an enclitic) verb, brought about when either an adverb was inserted before an "initial" verb, or an amplifying element was appended to a "final" verb. Schneider would like to completely separate the "original" clause-final verb from the later developed convention of placing the verb last in subordinate clauses, which he sees as being simply the result of the statistical preponderance of subordinate clauses which had pronominal subjects or objects. If we ignore the unfortunate political bias of Schneider's work, and look away from his contention that the initial verb was original, we may profitably examine the six clause types which he finds to be common to all the Germanic dialects. They are:

Type 1: Verb + Subject +...
Type 2: Nominal Subject + Verb +...
Type 3: Stressed word + Verb +...
Type 4: Particle + Verb + Subject +...
Type 5: Pronominal Subject + Verb +...
Type 6: Subject +...+ Verb

Schneider assumes[25] Types 1, 2, 3 and 6 to be Indo-European, and 4 and 5 to be Proto-Germanic innovations. If we accept Wackernagel's Law, we may combine Schneider's Types 2 and 3 into one type consisting of HEAVY ELEMENT + VERB. We then have the three positions of the verb — initial, second (enclitic) and final — described by Delbrück[26] for both Proto-Indo-European and Proto-Germanic. Schneider's work provides material, if not theoretical, support for Delbrück's hypothesis. We may, with Schneider,[27] see in Types 4 and 5, in which light elements precede the verb, special Germanic developments of the verb-initial clause. With these modifications, then, and with reservations about positing the initial verb as the normal Proto-Indo-European and Proto-Germanic order and about assuming different origins for Schneider's Type 6 clause and the verb-final subordinate clause, I find myself in substantial agreement with many of Schneider's conclusions.

2. *Indo-European Syntax*

In his article "Über ein Gesetz der indogermanischen Wortstellung", Wackernagel described the syntax of enclitic particles and pronouns in the earliest Indo-European

[25] Schneider, *Die Stellungtypen*, pp. 14 and 66.
[26] See below, p. 20.
[27] Schneider, *Die Stellungtypen*, pp. 37 and 40.

dialects. He observed that the enclitics were found consistently in the second position in the clause, immediately following the first autonomous word in the clause. Wackernagel also noted that if both enclitic particles and enclitic pronouns were present, the particles preceded the pronouns.[28] In the same article, Wackernagel discussed evidence that certain unemphatic verbs, such as *to be* and *to make*, were frequently found in the second position, and that unstressed verbs could have the same syntactic properties as enclitics.

Delbrück, in his work on comparative Indo-European syntax,[29] suggested further syntactic patterns for Proto-Indo-European. He assumed that the neutral sentence had the verb in the final position, but that certain undefined heavy elements could follow the verb.[30] (In 1959 Gonda described the nature of these heavy elements: they were amplificatory, that is, the sentence without them contained all the necessary grammatical components.[31]) Under conditions of emphasis (so-called *okkasionell* order) the verb could appear in the initial position or in a modification of it, the covered (*gedeckt*) initial position. The covered initial position was a variant of the initial position in which the verb was preceded by a particle only. Delbrück surmised that the initial position of the verb was used when a sentence formed part of an active narrative sequence, and in certain specialized functions such as interrogatives and imperatives. There were, then, two types of verb position: "The verb stood at the end in independent statement clauses and was weakly accented. If it was especially important, it came at the head of the clause and was strongly accented."[32] Delbrück later admitted a third possibility, the enclitic or second position.

One further positional constant was discovered for Proto-Indo-European, that of the preverb.[33] If the verb was compounded with a preverb, final position of the verb was obligatory, and two possible positions were available for the preverb in a main clause: either it stood at the head of the clause, followed by enclitics and separated from the verb by the rest of the clause (so-called tmesis), or else it was placed immediately before the unaccented main-clause verb. In subordinate clauses it was unaccented and attached proclitically to the accented verb. We may cite Vedic illustrations of the three types of position. For the preverb in a subordinate clause and the main clause contact type:

> *yebho mádhu pradhávati, tam cid eva ápi gacchatāt*
> 'those for whom the honey flows, those too shall join (them)' (*RV* X, 154, 2)

---

[28]   Wackernagel, "Über ein Gesetz":336.
[29]   Delbrück, *Vergleichende Syntax*, all three volumes.
[30]   Delbrück, *Vergleichende Syntax*, vol. III, 63.
[31]   Jan Gonda, *Four Studies in the Language of the Veda* (s'Gravenhage, Mouton, 1959), pp. 7-8.
[32]   Delbrück, *Vergleichende Syntax*, vol. III, p. 83.
[33]   Giuliano Bonfante, "Proposizione principale e proposizione dipendente in indoeuropeo", *Archivio Glottologico Italiano* 24 (1930). 2:41-42; cf. also Calvert Watkins, "Preliminaries to a Historical and Comparative Analysis of the Syntax of the Old Irish Verb", *Celtica* 6 (1963): 37-38.

For tmesis:

> *ápa tye tā́yave yathā́ nakṣatrā́ yanti áktubhiḥ*
> 'away go those stars like robbers, with their beams' (*RV* I, 50, 3)

The discovery of the Anatolian languages, which came after Wackernagel and Delbrück had begun the reconstruction of Proto-Indo-European syntax, not only confirmed Wackernagel's Law, but also permitted a more detailed description of the use and positional features of the particles and pronouns. Of especial interest is the use of sentence connectives such as Hittite *nu*, *ta* and *su*, Luwian *a*, and the phenomenon of sentence-initial conglomerates of a stressed particle followed by a string of particles and pronouns.[34] In a paper published in 1947, Dillon compared the Hittite sentence-connective *nu* with the Old Irish 'infixing' preverb *no-*, and suggested that the Hittite sequences of *nu* and enclitic pronouns were to be equated with the Old Irish pattern NO — ENCLITIC PRONOUNS — VERB.[35] Building on the work of Dillon and of Delbrück and others, Watkins proposed in 1962 and 1963 the reconstruction of a number of Proto-Indo-European sentence-types. The elements Watkins dealt with were: the finite verb (V), enclitics (E), which could be particles or pronouns, sentence connectives (N), preverbs (P) and a relativising particle (R). The possible sentence-types were then as follows:

$$
\begin{array}{lll}
\text{Compound Verb:} & \#P(E)\ldots & V\# \\
& \#\_\_(E)\ldots & PV\# \\
& \#N(E)\ldots & PV\# \\
\text{Simple Verb:} & \#\_\_(E)\ldots & V\# \\
& \#N(E)\ldots & V\# \\
& \#V(E)\ldots & \# \\
\end{array}
$$

The relativising particle R could appear either as N or as E, and should perhaps not be considered a separate element. The finite verb itself could also be enclitic, but Watkins' study includes only a tentative discussion of the enclitic verb. Watkins also omits discussion of the ordering of adverbials and nominal elements, such as subject, complement, direct and indirect object, except insofar as they are pronouns.

I will conclude this brief account of research in Indo-European and Germanic syntax with a summary of the main achievements. For Proto-Indo-European we may add to the sentence-types proposed by Watkins a main-clause sentence-type in which the verb is placed after the first autonomous element; the evidence adduced by Wackernagel[36] suggests that this second, so-called enclitic position of the verb, which is unimportant for Old Irish and is therefore ignored in Watkins' study of the historical syntax of the Old Irish verb[37], was present in Proto-Indo-European, and gained ground in several of the dialects, including Germanic. Of the studies of Germanic syntax,

[34] E. Laroche, "Comparaison du louvite et du lycien", *BSL* 53 (1958):168.
[35] Myles Dillon, "Celtic and the Other Indo-European Languages", *TPhS* 1947:23.
[36] Wackernagel, "Über ein Gesetz".
[37] Watkins, "Old Irish Verb".

Fourquet's is perhaps the most thorough, but has the drawback of lacking a concise statement on the syntax of the PROTO-Germanic sentence. Furthermore, Fourquet's conclusions are drawn solely from extrapolation from a number of synchronic descriptions.[38] As I shall try to show in the next section, this procedure is not sound because of the great number of possibilities available; there is no model beside which one may check one's conclusions. Yet Fourquet's series of synchronic descriptions have provided invaluable data for the present study. Kuhn's work has emphasized the positional features of the particles in Germanic sentences, and confirmed their tendency to be placed at or near the beginning of the clause.[39] On the position of the verb in the Proto-Germanic sentence scholars have agreed to some extent: the second position of the verb was possible in all the early Germanic languages; the verb's position varied according to whether the clause contained nouns or pronouns; in a subordinate clause the verb had a tendency to be placed at or near the end of the clause; in questions and imperatives the verb was usually at the head of the clause.

C. SOME METHODOLOGICAL CONSIDERATIONS

Meillet states: "the order of words had an expressive, not a syntactic value; it belonged to rhetoric, not to grammar."[40] Hirt also suggested that "the word order of Indo-European was to all appearances free",[41] but observed that a number of habitual patterns could be described.

The idea that Indo-European surface constituent, or word, order was 'free' has been pervasive, and yet there has been almost no conscious consideration of the general linguistic implications of the concept of free word order. Firstly, free word order has never been held to mean complete anarchy. When Hirt illustrates free word order by quoting the line from Horace: *aequam memento arduis in rebus servare mentem*, he does not mention the fact that the order of preposition and governed noun *in rebus* is immutable in Latin, nor does he point out the highly stylized and artificial balancing of words (adjective and noun straddling the sentence at opposite ends, verb and dependent infinitive enclosing the noun phrase, etc.). Even where a high degree of flexibility is found in word order, it seems that both stylistic and grammatical constraints exist also. Where free (or relatively free) word order is present, it does not mean that an author has arbitrarily 'scrambled' surface constituents. There may be several reasons for a particular rearrangement. The word order chosen may reflect pure metrical convenience, if the medium is poetry. It may be in obedience to stylistic conventions (variety or some other acknowledged standard of rhetoric). It may be

[38] Fourquet, *L'Ordre*.
[39] Kuhn, "Zur Wortstellung".
[40] Antoine Meillet, *Introduction à l'étude comparative des langues indo-européennes*, 8ème ed. (Paris, Hachette, 1937), p. 365.
[41] Hermann Hirt, *Indogermanische Grammatik, V-VII Teile* (Heidelberg, Winter, 1929-36), vol. VII, p. 142.

linguistically constrained through the contingencies of old and new information (thematic and rhematic material); the word order of Czech, for example, has been shown to be sensitive to this distinction.[42]

Secondly, it has not been proven that because many of the Indo-European languages have or had flexible word order, this situation must also have prevailed in Proto-Indo-European. The 'free' word order situation could conceivably have arisen spontaneously in separate dialects. If this is so, then an inspection of the more usual and neutral (stylistically unmarked) word-orders in the dialects could give evidence of an earlier more rigid word order. Thus, I shall attempt to show that in the early Germanic dialects there is evidence of a prior stage with verb-final word order, a situation which is also recoverable from Latin, Sanskrit and Hittite. The increasing flexibility which becomes apparent during the 'classical' phases of many Indo-European languages is susceptible of explanation as a 'drift' of the Western languages of the family away from the rigid syntactic type represented by the SOV languages towards the SVO type (Types III and II respectively in the Greenberg syntactic typology).[43] For example, in early Latin many of the surface characteristics of SOV (Type III) languages are to be found: postpositions rather than prepositions; the order of genitive and noun is GN; comparatives are formed with the order *illo fortior*, 'braver than him', i.e., with the order STANDARD — (MARKER) — ADJECTIVE; and the verb is almost invariably in the final position. By the period of the early Romance dialects, this situation is almost reversed. The verb appears invariably between the subject and the object, the genitive follows the noun, prepositions only are found, and so on. Some general typological shift has occurred, the reasons for which are unclear, although *a priori* one would suspect an areal linguistic influence.[44] The important thing is that free word order, or highly flexible word order, need not be considered as a phenomenon in some sense 'genetically' characteristic of a particular family, but rather as a general intermediate stage which accompanies a diachronic change in typological affiliation. We can EXPECT, therefore, that when a language changes from the rigid Type III (SOV) to Type II (SVO), it will pass through a stage in which alternative word orders are grammatically possible, though presumably with different expressive values. The attribute of free word order in even a wide variety of daughter-languages does not mean that the proto-language also possessed this attribute. The proto-language could have been a representative of a different linguistic type. If so, then this fact should be recoverable from an examination of the possible word-order patterns of the daughter-languages.

Of these word-order patterns, some will be expressive or will have special functions (imperative, interrogative, etc.), and some can perhaps be regarded as 'neutral'

---

[42]   See the discussion and bibliography in Joseph Vachek, *The Linguistic School of Prague: An Introduction to its Theory and Practice* (Bloomington, Indiana University Press, 1966), and especially, pp. 88-95.

[43]   Cf. Greenberg, ed., *Universals*, pp. 73-113.

[44]   Cf. pp. 95-96.

(unmarked). If these neutral word-orders could be readily identified, the problem of drawing general conclusions from word order patterns would be greatly simplified. As it is, however, limitations on the availability of longer texts, and distortions of these texts through foreign influences and stylistic effects permit of only tentative conclusions. One can identify certain styles and genres in which neutral word orders are likely to occur, such as factual narrative not characterized by lively action and rapidly moving events, statements in which no constituent has contrastive focus, and perhaps others.

Text which are translations from Latin or Greek may also provide information about 'favoured' sentence-types. If (as for example in Wulfila's Gothic Bible translation) the translator's technique has been to reproduce faithfully the sequence of the original rather than to express the ideas of the *Vorlage* in the target language, then departures from the sequence of the *Vorlage* may give information about word orders which were impossible in the target language. Such departures could come about if a single word in the *Vorlage* required several words for its rendering, as well as when the order in the *Vorlage* was unintelligible in the target language.

The constituents whose relative ordering inside the sentence will be considered here are those which figure in traditional syntactic studies of Germanic and Indo-European: PARTICLES and PRONOUNS, the class of metrically 'light' elements; the VERBAL COM-PLEX, consisting of the finite verb and the elements clustered around it — the PREVERB, PARTICIPLES, PARTICLES OF NEGATION, and REFLEXIVE; ADVERBIALS, ADJECTIVES and NOUNS (the larger class of metrically 'heavy' elements).

D. SOURCES

Secondary sources are referred to in the footnotes and Bibliography. Primary sources for the materials in the older Germanic dialects are as follows:

Old English, including the *Anglo-Saxon Chronicle* (referred to as *Chronicle*), *Beowulf*, *Andreas*, *The Dream of the Rood* (referred to as *Rood*), *The Battle of Maldon* and *The Wanderer*:

    Charles Plummer, *Two of the Saxon Chronicles, Parallel...* Friedrich Klaeber, *Beowulf, and the Fight at Finnsburg* W. F. Bolton, ed., *An Old English Anthology* (*Rood. The Battle of Maldon* and *The Wanderer*)

    Kenneth R. Brooks, ed., *Andreas, and the Fates of the Apostles*

Old Saxon, including *Heliand*:

    Otto Behaghel, *Heliand und Genesis*

Old High German, including *Hildebrandslied*, *Muspilli*, Isidor, *Contra Iudeos*, and Otfrid, *Evangelienbuch* (referred to as Otfrid):

    Wilhelm Braune, *Althochdeutsches Lesebuch* (*Hildebrandslied*, *Contra Iudeos* and *Muspilli*)

    Johann Kelle, *Otfrid von Weissenburg Evangelienbuch*

Gothic, including the following books of the New Testament; *Matthew, Mark, Luke, John, Romans, Corinthians, Galatians, Thessalonians*:

> Wilhelm Streitberg, ed., *Die Gotische Bibel*

Old Norse, including *Vafþrúðnismal, Libellus Islandorum, Heimskringla, Morkinskinna*, and *Hávamál*:

> E. V. Gordon, *An Introduction to Old Norse*
> Andreas Heusler, *Altisländisches Elementarbuch*
> Gustav Neckel, *Edda*

Footnotes indicate which primary source has been used for each quotation.

Runic Monuments, including *Kjølevik Stone, Freilaubersheimer Stone, Etelheim Bracelet, Vetteland Stone, Bø Stone, Tomstad Stone, Räsval Stone, Valsfjörd Rock Inscription, Veblungnes Rock Inscription*:

> Wolfgang Krause and Herbert Jankuhn, *Die Runeninschriften im Älteren Futhark*

Old Swedish, including some old Swedish laws:

> Berthold Delbrück, *Die Wortstellung in dem älteren westgötischen Landrecht*
> Elias Wessén, *Fornsvenska Texter*

Footnotes indicate which primary source has been used for each quotation.

Hittite, including *Hattusilis*:

> Edgar Sturtevant and George Bechtel, *A Hittite Chrestomathy*

Sanskrit, including *Rig-Veda* (referred to as *RV*):

> Theodor Aufrecht, *Die Hymnen des Rig-Veda*

Full Bibliographical information on all primary sources may be found in the Bibliography.

Except for the Hittite passage on pp. 28-29, all translations into English are the author's.

The sources for citations from other Indo-European languages are given in the body of the text.

In this study, considerable attention is given to the evidence of the earlier portions of the *Anglo-Saxon Chronicle*. This text has long been the object of study by scholars interested in the sentence structure of early Germanic. The reasons for this are the relative uniformity of the earlier parts; its apparently unadulterated nature (it does not seem to be a translation, as are many Old English prose works); its antiquity, in that it represents an unusually large corpus of running narrative text dating from the ninth century; the excellent condition of the manuscript, which is contemporary with the time of composition;[45] and, not least, the fascination of apparently insoluble problems which confront the investigator in attempting to impose order on the seemingly chaotic syntactic patterns found in this text. It should be mentioned here that I make no claims to have solved these and many other riddles associated with the syntax of the *Chronicle*; on the contrary, I am painfully aware that the generalizations

---

[45] For these points, cf. Ann Shannon, *A Descriptive Syntax of the Parker Manuscript of the Anglo-Saxon Chronicle from 734 to 891* (The Hague, Mouton, 1964), p. 7.

I have made are capable in many instances of contradiction from the same work. It is rather as a specimen of GERMANIC prose that I have approached the *Chronicle*. The many individual peculiarities of OLD ENGLISH syntax still require very much investigation.

II

THE SYNTAX OF THE PARTICLES AND PRONOUNS

A. SECTION I: THE PARTICLES

1. *General Remarks*

The Indo-European sentence elements known as particles belong to the class of FUNCTION words, which indicate grammatical relationships between the constituents of a clause. The study of particles is therefore essentially syntactic rather than morphological, a fact which has no doubt contributed to the inadequate treatment they were accorded until recent times. Streitberg does not mention them at all in the *Urgermanische Grammatik*, and Hirt concludes his discussion by describing the whole area as of little value for comparative studies.[1]

If we consider the reflexes of an Indo-European particle in the dialects, it is indeed difficult to make a useful comparative statement. The typical particle is composed of one or two phonemes only, and its function in a later stage of a dialect often bears little resemblance to its presumable original function. For example, the Proto-Indo-European particle *u* was enclitic and probably served as an intensifier.[2] In Gothic the particle *u* is an interrogative marker. If the two are etymologically identical, we have to assume a development from an intensifying to an interrogating function. On the other hand, the early Germanic dialects all had a relativizing particle: Gothic *ei*, Old English *the*, Old High German *the*, Old Norse *es*, but these particles are derived from several different Proto-Indo-European stems.

With the particles, then, we may have etymological identity and functional divergence, and also functional identity without a phonological equation. There are further a few examples where a complete parallel — functional, phonological and syntactical — can be drawn between a Proto-Indo-European particle and its Germanic reflex. In my treatment of the particles I will be concerned mainly with functional

---

[1] Wilhelm Streitberg, *Urgermanische Grammatik*, 3rd ed. (Heidelberg, Winter, 1963); Hermann Hirt, *Handbuch des Urgermanischen* (Heidelberg, Winter, 1931-32) vol. III, p. 192.
[2] Karl Brugmann, *Kurze vergleichende Grammatik der indogermanischen Sprache. Auf Grund des fünfbändigen "Grundrisses... von K. Brugmann und B. Delbrück" verfasst* (Berlin and Leipzig, de Gruyter, 1902-04), p. 617.

and positional features, rather than etymological ones, and will introduce etymological evidence only when it is of especial interest.

2. *The Sentence Connectives*

In Proto-Indo-European a number of particles served the function of joining together sentences in series. Presumably each particle so used had a slightly different nuance. There was a neutral sentence connective, which showed that the sentence following it was linked to the preceding sentence. Other sentence connectives may have indicated a more precise connection between the two clauses. There was undoubtedly also at least one relativizing particle.

The position in the clause of the sentence-connectives in Proto-Indo-European was constant. They were either initial and accented or unaccented and attached to the first autonomous word in the clause (Wackernagel's Law). The positional characteristics are, however, perhaps of less interest, in that the head or near-head position is a natural one for elements having the function of joining a clause to a preceding clause.[3] An example of an accented particle in initial position is the Vedic particle *átha*, as, for example, in *marúdbhir indra sakhyáṁ te astu áthemā víçvāḥ pŕtanā jayāsi* 'be friends with the Maruts, o Indra, and you shall win all battles' (*RV* 8, 85, 2). In Hittite and other Anatolian languages a frequently occurring pattern is a clause-initial connective having a string of particles and pronouns attached to it, or with another word at the head of the sentence and enclitic particles and pronouns attached to that word. Examples from Hittite[4] are (with initial particle) *na-as-mu-kan* 'and, she, me, thither' (*Hattusilis* 3); *nu-wa-za-kan* 'and, direct speech, reflexive, thither, (*Hattusilis* 12); (with word other than particle in initial position) *u-it-ma* 'came however' (*Hattusilis* 7); *DISTAR-mu-kan* 'Istar me forth' (*Hattusilis* 6). Watkins has suggested that such patterns existed in Proto-Indo-European.[5]

Proto-Germanic had reflexes of these patterns in the ordering of both connectives and pronouns. Both sentence-initial and enclitic connectives were present. In Gothic, for example, *iþ* 'but' and *jah* 'and', and in Old English *ond* 'and', are never enclitic; the two Gothic particles are placed at the head of the clause even when they translate Greek enclitics.[6] On the other hand, the Gothic particles *u* 'interrogative particle' and *uh* 'and; intensifier' are enclitic. They are found only as the second element in a clause, and form a phonological unit with the word which they follow: a word-final spirant is not devoiced before a following enclitic, e.g., *miþ iddjedun* 'they accompanied' (*Luke* 14, 15) but *uz-uh-iddja* 'and he went out' (*John* 16, 28).[7]

---

[3] Cf. Kuhn, "Zur Wortstellung": p. 5.
[4] Hittite examples are by selection and paragraph number in Edgar Sturtevant and Bechtel, *A Hittite Chrestomathy* (Philadelphia, Linguistic Society of America, 1935).
[5] Calvert Watkins, "Preliminaries to the Reconstruction of Indo-European Sentence Structure", in *Proceedings of the 9th International Congress of Linguists* (The Hague, Mouton, 1964) 1035-42.
[6] Fourquet, *L'ordre*, p. 246.
[7] Antoine Meillet, "Notes sur quelques faits gothiques", *MSL* 15 (1908-09):95-97.

From the comparative evidence it may be assumed that Proto-Indo-European had a neutral sentence-connective which appeared with great regularity in every sentence which in any way continued the topic of the preceding one. A particle having such a function is found in many of the oldest dialects: Old Latin *que*, Greek δε, Hittite *nu*, with the very oldest Hittite texts showing *su* and *ta*. Such particles were especially common in extended narrative sequences.

In the Old English *Chronicle* the successive events of a year are regularly introduced by the particle *ond* (normally written '7'). The similarity between this usage and the use of *nu* in running text in Hittite is very striking; the *Chronicle* is shown by it to preserve as perhaps no other Germanic monument a syntactic feature of Proto-Indo-European narrative language. The Parker Manuscript entry for the year 871 A.D. gives a good idea of the use of *ond*.

7 þæs ymb .xiiii. niht gefeaht Æþered cyning 7 Ælfred his broþur wiþ þone here æt Basengum' 7 þær þa Deniscan sige namon; 7 þæs ymb .ii. monaþ gefeaht Æþered cyning 7 Ælfred his broþur wiþ þone here æt Mere tune, 7 hie wærun on tuæm gefylcium, 7 hie butu gefliemdon, 7 longe on dæg sige ahton, 7 þær wearþ micel wæl sliht on gehwæþere hond, 7 þa Deniscan ahton wæl stowe geweald; 7 þær wearþ Heahmund bisc: ofslægen, 7 fela godra monna; 7 æfter þissum gefeohte cuom micel sumor lida; 7 þæs ofer Eastron gefor Æþered cyning, 7 he ricsode .v. gear, 7 his lic liþ æt Winburnan. (*Chronicle* 871 A.D.)

þa feng Ælfred Æþelwulfing his broþur to Wesseaxna rice; 7 þæs ymb anna monaþ gefeaht Ælfred cyning wiþ alne þone here lytle werede æt Wiltune, 7 hine longe on dæg gefliemde, 7 þa Deniscan ahton wæl stowe gewald; 7 þæs geares wurdon .viii. folc gefeoht gefohten wiþ þone here on þy cynerice be suþan Temese, 7 butan þam þe him Ælfred þæs cyninges broþur, 7 anlipig aldor-mon, 7 þæs cyninges þegnas oft rade onridon þe mon na ne rimde, 7 þæs geares wærun ofslægene .viiii. eorlas 7 an cyning; 7 þy geare namon West Seaxna friþ wiþ þone here.

'And a fortnight later King Ethelred and his brother Alfred fought against the Danish army at Basingham, and there the Danes won a victory. And two months later King Ethelred and his brother Alfred fought against the Danish army at Merton, and they were in two regiments, and they put them both to flight, and held off their counter-attacks all day, and on both sides there was great slaughter, but the Danes won the day. And Bishop Heahmund was slain there, and many good men. After this battle a great summer army arrived. And over Easter King Ethelred died. He reigned five years, and his body lies at Winburn.

Then his brother Alfred, son of Ethelwolf, succeeded to the kingdom of Wessex. And a month later King Alfred fought against the entire Danish army with a small band of men, and held them off for a long time during the day, but the Danes won the field. During this year seven general engagements were fought against the Danish army in Surrey, not to mention those which Alfred, the King's brother, a single alderman and the king's thanes most frequently rode out on, and which no one ever counted. During this year eight earls and one king were killed. And in the same year the West Saxons made a treaty with the Danish army'.

Beside this passage I give a sample of Hittite text to illustrate the use of *nu*.

nu KUR.UGU-*TI* ta-par-ha pi-ra-an-ma-at-mu ᴵ ᴰ*SIN*. ᴰU-as DUMU ᴵ*ZI-DA-A* ma-ni-ya-ah-hi-es-ki-it nu-mu ᴰ*ISTAR* GASAN-*YA* ku-it ka-ni-es-sa-an har-ta SES-*YA*-ya-mu ᴵNIR. GAL-is a-as-su har-ta nu-mu-kan GIM-an UKU.MES-an-na-an-za *SA* ᴰ*ISTAR* GASAN-*YA* ka-ni-es-su-u-wa-ar *SA* SES-*YA*-ya a-as-su-la-an a-u-e-ir nu-mu ar-sa-ni-i-e-ir nu-mu ᴵ ᴰ*SIN*. ᴰU-as DUMU ᴵ*ZI-DA-A* nam-ma-ya da-ma-a-us UKU.MES-us u-wa-a-i-ti-is-ki-u-wa-an ti-i-e-ir nu-mu-kan hu-u-wa-ap-pi-ir nu-mu ar-pa-sa-at-ta-be (nu)-mu SES-*YA* ᴵNIR.GALis *A-NA* ᴳᴵˢDUBBIN lam-ni-ya-at. (*Hattusilis* 4)

'Then I governed the Upper Country. Before me, however, Armadattas, son of Zidas, had been ruling it. Now because My Lady Istar had favored me and my brother Muwattallis was well disposed toward me, when people saw My Lady Istar's favor toward me and my brother's kindness, they envied me. And Armadattas, son of Zidas, and other men began to stir up ill will against me. They brought malice against me, and I had bad luck; and my brother Muwattallis named me for the wheel (?)'

In Gothic we often find that clauses in paratactic coordination have the particle *uh* attached to the first word even when the original Greek does not provide a precedent:

> *jah usstigun in skip, iddjedun-uh ufar marein*
> καὶ ἀναβάντες εἰς τὸ πλοῖον ἤρχοντο...
> 'And they embarked on the boat and went over the lake' (*John* 6, 17)
>
> *manageins filu iddja du imma, qaþ-uh du Filippan*
> ὄχλος πολὺς ἔρχεται πρὸς αὐτόν λέγει πρὸς τὸν Φίλιππον
> 'A large crowd came to him, and he said to Philip' (*John* 6, 5)

On the other hand, Greek καὶ and δε are usually rendered by *jah* and *iþ*. The particle *uh* was apparently felt to be necessary in clauses in which no other sentence-connective stood.

Gothic *uh* is cognate with Latin *que*, which is also an enclitic connective. In the earliest Latin narrative texts, *que* functions as an almost obligatory sentence-connective introducing every clause, similar to Old English *ond* and Hittite *nu*.[8]

Proto-Germanic, then, had sentence-joining particles both of the clause-initial and enclitic kind, whose presence was virtually required in a clause in a narrative sequence. These particles added little or nothing to the lexical import of the clause, but simply characterized the clause as one which was part of the same series as the preceding clauses. With Gothic *uh* it is possible to propose a complete parallel — functional, syntactic and phonological — with the early Latin *que*. The etymology of Old English *ond* is too uncertain to make a phonological equation outside Germanic, but it has a syntactic and functional similarity to Hittite *nu*.

The reflex of the Proto-Indo-European particle *to* (Old Church Slavonic *ta*, Hittite *ta*) in Proto-Germanic served to mark a clause which introduced a new fact, in other words, to introduce a new sequence of sentences. I shall suggest in a later chapter that such sequence-initial sentences often had the verb in first position. A typical Germanic syntagm is therefore a clause-initial verb preceded by *þa*. In the *Chronicle* entry for the year 871 A.D., for example, the break with the preceding sequence is shown not only by the use of *þa*, but also by a new line in the manuscript:

7 þæs ofer Eastron gefore Æþered cyning, 7 he ricsode .v. gear, 7 his lic liþ æt Win burnam. þa feng Ælfred Æþelwulfing his broþur to Wesseaxna rice. (*Chronicle* 871 A.D.)
'And over Easter King Ethelred died. He reigned five years, and his body lies at Winburn. Then his brother Alfred, son of Ethelwolf, succeeded to the kingdom of Wessex'

As in Proto-Indo-European, the particle *nu* appears in Germanic in both a stressed and an enclitic form. In Gothic its function is 'conclusive' (glossed by Krause "nun, daher, also"[9]), which accords with Sturtevant's suggestion that the original 'Indo-Hittite' value of **nu* was to introduce a "logical inference rather than a new item in

---

8 Cf. Watkins, "Irish Verb": 8-9.
9 Wolfgang Krause, *Handbuch des Gotischen* (München, Beck, 1953), p. 199.

the narrative."[10] As an enclitic it may have had a similar function, as in Gothic *us-nu-gibiþ*, ἀπόδοτε τοίνυν, 'render therefore' (*Luke* 20, 25), or it may be merely an emphatic particle, as in exclamations such as Old High German *wola-nu, wolaga-nu,* Old English *heo-nu,* Old Saxon *si-nu,* '*ecce*'. Like its Hittite cognate, *nu* also supports enclitics, e.g., Gothic *nauh* 'yet' (**nu-kᵚe*), *nu-sai* 'νυνι', Old English *nu-þa*.[11]

3. *Relativizing Particles*

Proto-Germanic differed from many other Indo-European dialects in that it did not develop a paradigm of pronouns specialized for relativization. Instead, a relative clause was made either by simple juxtaposition of two clauses, a syntagm retained by most of the modern Germanic dialects, or by the use of a special particle.

In the use of particles rather than pronouns to introduce relative clauses, Proto-Germanic may have retained a feature even more archaic than most of the other dialects. It could, of course, be objected that Proto-Germanic has innovated; but relative pronouns, which can easily be analyzed as consisting of a particle either with a pronominal ending or with an enclitic pronoun attached to them, seem to represent a later, compound stage. Relativization by means of particles is usual in Old Irish, for example,[12] a dialect which has many archaic features.

The phonemic shape of the relativizing particle is not reconstructable for Proto-Germanic; yet in the modern dialects the form of the relative particles has been considerably altered in historical times, so that one is not surprised to find divergence even in the earliest written records.

In Gothic the enclitic particle *ei* is attached to a demonstrative pronoun, giving a paradigm *sa-ei, so-ei, pat-ei* etc. Gothic *ei* could also be combined with personal pronouns of the first and second person, giving combinations such as *ik-ei, þu-ei.* But whereas in Gothic particle and pronoun had already fused into a relative pronoun, in Old English and in Old Norse the two elements are still separate. In Old English, *cuius* is rendered by constructions such as:

> Karles sunu, þe Æþelwulf West Seaxna cyning his dohtor hæfde him to cuene
> 'the son of Charles, whose daughter Ethelwulf, King of the West Saxons, had as his wife' (*Chronicle* 885 A.D.)

Similar constructions can be cited for Old Norse.

> konungr gaf Hǫkone suerþ, þat er hiǫlten vǫró ór gulle
> 'the king gave Hagen a sword whose hilt was of gold'[13]

---

[10]   Edgar Sturtevant, *A Comparative Grammar of the Hittite Language*, vol. I, with Adelaide E. Hahn (New Haven, Yale University Press, 1951), p. 108. Cf. Paul J. Hopper, "An Indo-European 'Syntagm' in Germanic", *Linguistics* 54 (1969).

[11]   Friedrich Kluge, *Urgermanisch: Vorgeschichte der altgermanischen Dialekte*, 3rd ed. (Strassburg, Trübner, 1913), p. 97.

[12]   Rudolf Thurneysen, *A Grammar of Old Irish, Revised and Enlarged Edition, Translated from the German by D. A. Binchy and Osborn Bergin* (Dublin, Institute for Advanced Studies, 1961), pp. 312-25.

[13]   Andreas Heusler, *Altisländisches Elementarbuch*, 4th ed. (Heidelberg, Winter, 1950), p. 160.

And other oblique cases are formed identically, such as *quibus*.

> Nis nu cwicra nan
> þe ic him modsefan minne durre
> sweotule asecgan (*The Wanderer* 9-11)
>
> 'There is now none alive to whom I dare openly tell my thoughts'

In many of the modern spoken dialects particles are also in more common use than pronouns, for example the Southern German *wo*, British English *as*. In Danish the particle *som* is used except in the genitive (*hvis*).[14]

B. SECTION II: THE PRONOUNS

In Proto-Indo-European, pronouns, like particles, could be autonomous or enclitic. Both kinds are found in the early Germanic dialects. The syntax of the enclitics in Proto-Indo-European was described by Wackernagel,[15] and has been amply confirmed by the evidence of the Anatolian languages: the unaccented elements were placed near the head of the clause, immediately following the first autonomous word. Laroche describes the Hittite and Luwian clause as follows:

> The Hittite clause is dominated by an initial accented word to which is attached a greater or lesser number of enclitics. The first word is either an appellative of some kind or a particle...The Luwian clause offers a comparable structure.[16]

If a clause contained enclitic particles and enclitic pronouns, the particles preceded the pronouns in Proto-Indo-European.[17]

In this section I will treat enclitic and non-enclitic pronouns separately. Proto-Germanic did not, however, inherit a special set of enclitic pronouns distinct from non-enclitic ones, but rather it inherited the pattern of enclisis. The difference between enclitic and non-enclitic pronouns in the Germanic dialects is therefore a syntactic rather than a morphological or phonological one.

In the early Germanic languages the use of a pronominal subject was probably usual; the omission of the pronoun is sporadic in original texts, especially poetic ones, and it is only in works which adhere closely to a Greek or Latin model that the subject is frequently left unexpressed. In Gothic, as Meillet has shown,[18] there are many examples of pronouns added against the *Vorlage*, but almost no places where the

---

14   Consistent with the intended scope of the present study, the enormously complex problems of embedding constructions will not be dealt with here, and therefore no mention is made of rules concerning relativization. The examples just quoted, however, show that in Germanic relative clauses are positioned after the noun which they modify. If one excepts the possessive genitive and the adjective, which are presumably derived from reduced clauses, there are no traces in Germanic of preposed relative clauses.

15   Wackernagel, "Über ein Gesetz":336.

16   Laroche, "Louvite et Lycien":162.

17   Delbrück, *Vergleichende Syntax*, vol. III, 51.

18   Meillet, "Faits gothiques":89.

translator has failed to render a Greek pronoun. Meillet further observes that in all the Germanic dialects, through regular sound change, the first and third persons singular of the strong preterite are identical in form; yet not only does no dialect introduce a morphological innovation to differentiate the forms, but in some dialects still further syncretism has taken place. He concludes that the use of subject pronouns was general throughout the Germanic speaking areas.

1. *Non-Enclitic Pronouns*

The normal position of pronouns in the early Germanic dialects was at or near the beginning of the clause. Although patterns of pronouns immediately following an accented initial word are found only vestigially, even non-enclitic pronouns were placed toward the head of the sentence. Sentence elements which belonged together in the clause were often separated by the consistent arrangement of pronouns and other light elements in the initial position, so that, for example, a pronominal direct object may precede a subject noun. The following examples are taken from the earliest Old English narrative prose, the *Chronicle*:

> 7 him þa Carl Francna cyning his dohtor geaf
> 'and then Charles, King of the Franks, gave him his daughter' (*Chronicle* 855 A.D.)
>
> þa was domne Leo papa on Rome, 7 he hine to cyninge gehalgode, 7 hiene him to biscep suna nam
> 'at that time Lord Leo was Pope in Rome, and he consecrated him king, and adopted him as his godson at confirmation' (*Chronicle* 853 A.D.)
>
> 7 he hi him eft ageaf
> 'and he returned them to him' (*Chronicle* 894 A.D.)
>
> 7 he hie to æþmodre hersumnesse gedyde
> 'and he subjected them to humble obedience' (*Chronicle* 828 A.D.)
>
> 7 hie him alle ge hiersume dydon
> 'and they all did obedience to him' (*Chronicle* 853 A.D.)

There is a rather striking syntactic resemblance between the Hittite clause-initial clusters such as *na-an-mu-kan* 'and him to me thither' and Old English patterns such as *ond he hi him eft* 'and he them to him back', except that whereas in Hittite the pronouns and particles are in enclisis to the initial particle, in the Germanic dialects the pronouns and particles are autonomous elements which, although carrying very weak stress, did not stand in enclitic dependency to an initial particle.

In early Germanic alliterative verse pronouns are unstressed (that is, they almost never take part in alliteration), and frequently appear in anacrusis, among the unstressed elements preceding the alliterating word. The half-lines of alliterative verse usually comprise a complete phrase, and often a whole clause, of which the unstressed elements in anacrusis are the opening words. The following examples are from Old English, Old Saxon and Old Norse alliterative verse:

[19]   References to Old Norse verse (*Varfðrúðnismál*) are by selection and stanza in Gustav Neckel, *Edda. Die Lieder des Codex Regius nebst verwandten Denkmälern. I. Text. 3., umarbeitete Auflage von Hans Kuhn* (Heidelberg, Winter, 1962).

(te sulicun ambahtskepi), so he mi egan uuili (*Heliand* 284)
'if he wishes to have me'

(giuuendid after them uuordun), that he im to them uuiba genam (*Heliand* 330)
'that he betook himself to the woman'

Mundilfoeri heitir, hann er Mána faðir (*Vafðrūðnismal* 234)
'he is called Mundilfoeri, he is the Moon's father'

Segðu þat iþ átta, allz þic fróðan qveða,
          oc þú, Vafðrúðnir, vitir,
hvat þú fyrst mant... (*Vafðrūðnismal* 34)
'Tell me an eighth thing, since you are said to be wise, and must know it: what do you
first remember?'

Him þa Scyld gewat to gesceaphwile (*Beauulf* 26)
'Scyld departed at his fate time'

þa he him of dyde isernbyrnan (*Beauulf* 671)
'then he took off his steel corslet'

In the older Runic inscriptions non-enclitic pronouns, that is in effect pronouns
not immediately following the verb, are placed at the head of the clause. Amongst
those inscriptions whose interpretation is reasonably sure, I find the following examples
of pronouns occurring at the head.[20]

ek Hagusta(l)daR hl(a)aiwido magu minino
'I Hagustald buried my boy' (*Kjølevik Stone*)

þk Daþina golida
'Dathena greeted you' (*Freilaubersheimer Fibula*)

m(i)k M(e)r(i)la w(o)rte
'Merila wrought me' (*Etelhem Bracelet*)

2. *Enclitic Pronouns*

The few instances that can be cited of pronouns in enclisis to particles almost all have
the appearance of later formations. Kuhn lists some examples from Middle High
German: *swenner = swenne er*, *deich = daz ich*, *weiz = waz iz*, and Old Norse:
þottu = þot þu,[21] but none of these forms was inherited from Proto-Germanic.
There is, however, some indication that pronouns, like particles, could appear in
enclisis to sentence-initial particles in Proto-Germanic. Such enclitic patterns are found
only vestigially in the recorded dialects.

In Gothic enclitic particles are regularly placed in the second position in the clause,
even when the initial word is a particle, for example *þan-uh*: *þan-uh biþe ut usiddjedun
eis* 'but when they had gone out of them', αὐτῶν δὲ ἐξερχόμενων, (*Matthew* 9, 32).
Enclisis of particles to preverbs is especially frequent in Gothic, and in one instance
we find as many as three particles intervening between the first preverb and the verb:
gah-þan-miþ-sandidedun 'and they sent also' (*Corinthians* II, 8, 18). There is, however,

---

20   Text and interpretations are from Wolfgang Krause and Herbert Jan Kuhn, *Die Runeninschriften im älteren Futhark I*: Text (Gottingen, Vanderhoeck and Rubrecht, 1966), pp. 173, 283, 39,
respectively.
21   Kuhn, "Zur Wortstellung":89.

only one example of a pronoun in a similar syntactic position: *frah ina ga-u-hwa-sehwi* 'he asked him whether he saw anything' ἐπηρώτα αὐτὸν εἴ τι βλέπει (*Mark* 8, 23); yet, unique as this example is, it seems authentic. The number of occasions which would call for such a pattern is small in our only Gothic text (the *New Testament*, which favors direct rather than indirect speech). There are no occurrences at all of the indefinite pronoun *hwas* followed by the interrogative particle *u*. Only the verb or the preverb could support *u*, and the translator had the choice between the given pattern and *ga-u-sehwi-hwa* (*ga-sehwi-u* would be impossible, for the enclitic would then be in third place). Even though it is a hapax legomenon, the occurrence of *ga-u-hwa-sehwi* suggests that some pronouns could be attached enclitically to preverbs in Gothic. Although a single instance cannot be conclusive, we observe that the Indo-European order of enclitics: PARTICLE — PRONOUN is preserved.

The second Germanic syntagm which suggests that sentence-initial clusters of a particle and pronouns like those described for the Anatolian dialects by Laroche once existed in Proto-Germanic is the West Germanic use of the exclamatory particle *hwat*. In the fourth volume of the *Deutsche Grammatik*, Grimm discusses the syntax of this particle. He notes that it is placed at the head of a clause, especially to introduce direct speech, and that it always precedes pronouns. Although it is often translated by such words as *lo!*, *well!*, it frequently has no observable lexical meaning: "The Anglo-Saxon often uses it when no word of the original (Latin) text requires it."[22] In West Germanic alliterative verse *hwat* is often the first word of a passage in indirect speech, as in these examples from *Beowulf* and the *Heliand*:

> thar uualdand Crist
> obar that liudo folc lera sagde:
> "huat, ik iu seggean mag", quað he, "gesiðos mine" (*Heliand* 2388)
> 'where the Lord Christ told a parable to the people: "Lo, my friends, I will tell you" he said'
> endi tho te theme thegne sprac
> magad unuuanlic: "huat, thu mahtis man wesan" quaðsiu (*Heliand* 4957)
> 'and then the woman said roughly to the disciple: "You must be one of the men"'
> (hard heritogo:) "huat, gi mi thesan haftan man" quathie (*Heliand* 5314)
> '"You (sent) me this bound man" he said'
>
> Beowulf maþelode, bearn Ecgþeowes:
> "Hwæt, we þe þas sælac, sunu Healfdenes,
> leod Scyldinga, lustum brohton (*Beowulf* 1651-53)
> 'This sea-booty, o son of Healfdene, chief of the Scyldings, we have brought to you with joy'
> Beowulf maþelode, bearn Ecgþeowes:
> "Hwæt, þu worn fela, wine min Unfer,
> beore druncen ymbe Brecan spræce (*Beowulf* 529-31)
> 'You have said many things, my friend Unferth, about Breca, while you were drunk with beer'

It is frequently used in Old English to begin a poem, as for example in *Beowulf*:

> Hwæt, we Gar-Dena in geardagum (*Beowulf* 1)
> 'We the Spear-Danes in days of yore'

---

[22] Jacob Grimm, *Deutsche Grammatik*, 4. *Teil*: *Syntax*. (Gütersloh, Bertelsmann, 1898), p. 529.

and in the *Dream of the Rood* :

> Hwæt, ic swefna cyst secgan wylle (*Rood* 1)
> 'I will tell of the best of dreams'

It seems that pronouns were not felt to be sufficiently autonomous to provide the initial articulation of a series of clauses, but had to be reinforced by an accented particle, much as in Hittite enclitic pronouns were attached to an initially accented word. If *hwat* had a more emphatic stress than the following pronouns in Germanic, we would expect to find that at least sometimes it took part in alliteration. I have found no indication of *hwat* in alliteration in Old Saxon, but in two occurrences in *Beowulf* it shares the alliteration with another sound. They are:

> *H*wæt, we þe þas *s*ælac, *s*unu *H*ealfdenes (*Beowulf* 1652)
> Hwæt, me þæs on *e*þle *e*dwenden cwom (*Beowulf* 1774)
> 'in my country a change came to me from this'

(The alliteration is somewhat doubtful in the second example, but the metre requires a stress on *hwæt*). Apparently, therefore, *hwat* carried a heavier stress than the following pronouns, even though it only occasionally alliterates. It may be that the habit of inserting a word-boundary between *hwat* and the pronouns is a scribal convention of fairly recent date.[23]

Enclisis of pronouns to a verb is common in all the early Germanic dialects. But there is no evidence that special enclitic pronouns were inherited from Proto-Indo-European; where the shape of an enclitic pronoun in Germanic differs from that of a non-enclitic pronoun, the difference may always be attributed to weak stress and the close proximity to the final phoneme of the verb.[24] The Runic monuments, it is true, show a pronoun of the first person *(e)ka*, as in the *Lindholm Stone*: *ek erilaR sa wilagaR ha(i)teka* 'I the Eril here am called the Cunning One',[25] and Meillet assumed that *eka* was a special enclitic form. But more recently another inscription has been found, the *Söderköping Stone*, in which the same form is found non-enclitically: *eka sigimAr* "I Sigmar..."[26] The etyma of the pronouns *ek* and *eka*, Proto-Indo-European *eg* and *egom*, do not suggest that the longer form was enclitic. I give a selection of examples from the dialects of pronouns in enclisis to a verb: Old Norse *hefk* (*hef ek*), *skaltu* (*skalt þu*), *kallask* (*kallar sik*); Old English *wenic* (*wen ic*); Old High German *zelluh*, *zellih* (*zellu ih*), *beguolen* (*beguol inan*), *meg ih* (*mag ih*), *werf iz*

---

[23] The possibility of combining an exclamatory stem *k^wo- with a following word may even be of Indo-European date. In Sanskrit the particle *ka* may be prefixed to a noun or adjective to give either an appreciative, or depreciative value, e.g., *ko-vida* 'well knowing, skilled', *kā-purusa* 'miserable man, coward' (cf. William D. Whitney, *Sanskrit Grammar*, 2nd ed. (Leipzig, Breitkopf and Härtel, 1889), pp. 195 and 412). Although the usage is more frequent in the later language, it is known in Vedic Sanskrit. Cf. also Hirt, *Grammatik*, vol. VI, p. 53.

[24] Meillet, however, assumes ("Faits gothiques":90) two sets of pronouns, an enclitic and a non-enclitic, for Germanic, and accepts a Proto-Indo-European first person plural enclitic pronoun *mes* as the origin of the Old High German verbal ending -*mēs* ("Faits gothiques":91).

[25] From Krause and Jankuhn, *Die Runeninschriften*, p. 70.

[26] Krause and Jankuhn, *Die Runeninschriften*, p. 132.

(*warf iz*). Among the typical sandhi changes are those of *þ* to *t*, and, especially in Old High German, umlaut of the vowel of the verb root caused by the front vowel of the enclitic pronoun.

The question remains, under what circumstances did enclisis take place? Since the normal position for the pronouns in Proto-Germanic was at or near the beginning of the clause, the most likely locus of diffusion of the syntagm VERB — ENCLITIC is the verb-initial clause. Such clauses were probably more frequent in Proto-Germanic than in the recorded dialects, for they occurred not only in imperative and interrogative constructions, but also under certain other conditions which I shall discuss in a later chapter. Proto-Germanic in turn inherited the syntagm from Proto-Indo-European. In Hittite, for example, although the verb is normally in the final position, verb-initial clauses are also attested, and in them pronouns are suffixed to the verb much as in Germanic. The pattern is described by Dillon, who gives as examples *pesta-s* 'he gave', *pesta-n* 'he gave him', etc.[27]

C. CONCLUSIONS

The syntax of the particles and pronouns in Proto-Germanic shows many archaic features. Both enclitic and clause-initial particles were present in Proto-Germanic, and their positional characteristics resembled those of the particles in the earliest Indo-European dialects. Pronouns were placed at or near the head of the clause. They could appear in enclisis to verbs and, to a more limited extent, to a clause initial particle. Relative subordination took place by means of particles rather than pronouns, whereas even many of the most archaic Indo-European dialects developed specialized relative pronouns.

[27]   Dillon, "Celtic":23.

III

THE SYNTAX OF THE VERBAL COMPLEX

A. SECTION I: STRUCTURE OF THE VERBAL COMPLEX

The Proto-Germanic verbal complex consisted of a number of constituents grouped around the inflected part of the verb. These constituents were: the NON-FINITE VERB, which in periphrastic constructions carried the actual lexical meaning of the verb; the NEGATIVE PARTICLE *ni*; a PREVERB, which modified the lexical meaning of the verb; and a REFLEXIVE PRONOUN.

In this chapter I shall be concerned mainly with the syntax of the finite verb itself. I shall first, however, discuss the arrangement of those sentence constituents which belonged closely to the finite verb.

1. *The Reflexive Pronoun*

In Old Norse and Gothic the reflexive pronoun *sik* was placed immediately after the finite verb. In Gothic, reflexive verbs translating Greek middle verbs quite consistently show the order: verb–*sik*, e.g., *ushaihah sik*, ἀπήγξατο, 'he hanged himself' (*Matthew* 27, 5), and in Old Norse the enclitic reflexive was 'suffixed' to the verb to form a medio-passive, e.g., *kallask* (= *kalla sik*) 'is called'. In Old Saxon the reflexive *im* occurs near the beginning of the clause with the other pronouns, e.g.:

> endi im uppan them hleuue gisat
> diurlic drohtines bodo (*Heliand* 5805-06)
> 'and upon the tomb sat a glorious messenger of the Lord'

In Old English the singular reflexive pronoun *hine* is identical with the third person singular accusative pronoun *hine*, but the syntax of *hine* as a reflexive differs from that of the personal pronoun. In the earliest Old English narrative prose the reflexive *hine* is placed immediately before the rest of the verbal complex, while the personal pronoun occurs toward the head of the clause with the other pronouns, e.g., personal pronouns:

> oþ þæt hiene an swan of stang (*Chronicle* 755 A.D.)
> 'until a herdsman stabbed him' (755 A.D.)

> 7 he hine to cyninge ge halgode (*Chronicle* 853 A.D.)
> 'and he consecrated him king'

Reflexives:

> Her cometa se steorra hiene oþiewde (*Chronicle* 729 A.D.)
> 'In this year the star Comet showed itself'
> Her hiene bestæl se here into Werham (*Chronicle* 876 A.D.)
> 'In this year the Danish army stole into Wareham'

The plural pronoun *hie* has the same syntactic properties, e.g.:

> þæt hie nænig mon siþþan findan ne meahte (*Chronicle* 418 A.D.)
> 'that afterwards no one could find them'

But:

> 7 hie be him lifgendum hie gedældun (*Chronicle* 718 A.D.)
> 'and they parted from one another during their lifetime'

Close proximity to the verb, then, characterized the reflexive as distinct from the other personal pronouns, especially if the verb was in final or near-final position. In other respects it was probable that the position of the reflexive with respect to the verb was identical to that of other objects of the verb: it would appear before the verb in those dialects and under those circumstances where the order SUBJECT — OBJECT — VERB (SOV) was preserved, and would be placed after the verb under other conditions. Thus in Old English, where the archaic word-order SOV still prevailed, the usual order is REFLEXIVE — VERB, while in Gothic and Old Norse, where the order SVO was becoming, or had become, normal, the order is VERB — REFLEXIVE. It is surely significant that Old English, where the positional features of the reflexive pronoun are so clearly distinct from those of non-reflexive object pronouns, is, along with Old Saxon, the only dialect which has lost the morphological distinction between reflexive and non-reflexive. It could, of course, be argued that the word-order difference was 'therapeutic', and came about precisely because of the necessity to distinguish between the two types of pronoun. Yet a syntactic distinction of this kind would, from a synchronic point of view, only be possible if the pronouns were marked as distinct. We cannot say that it is the WORD ORDER itself which distinguishes the two pronouns; rather, the word order difference is a consequence of the distinction between two 'different' morphemes which happen to coincide in phonological shape. Phonological difference thus appears as a rather superficial thing, which could be abandoned, given the existence of another marker (the word order).

It is remarkable also that the positional distinction between reflexive and non-reflexive in Old English is characteristic only of the third person, the only person in which any ambiguity is possible; as in general in Indo-European only the third person has distinct reflexive forms. The phenomenon is a baffling one, inasmuch as the rule which 'clusters' pronouns at the beginning of the clause fails to apply to just those reflexive pronouns which might be confused with non-reflexives.[1]

---

[1] A solution on transformational lines would thus appear to be excluded.

2. *The Negative Particle*

The syntax of the negative particle in Germanic has been made the object of studies by Mourek[2] and Delbrück.[3] Mourek distinguished QUALITATIVE negation, in which the entire predicate of a judgment is negated, and QUANTITIVE negation, in which only one part of a judgment (e.g., the subject, object, circumstance, etc.) is negated.[4] In qualitative negation in Germanic, the particle *ni* is placed immediately before the finite verb, regardless of the position of the finite verb in the clause, for example:

> that thu giuuald obar mik
> hebbian ni mohtis (*Heliand* 5350-51)
> 'that you cannot have any power over me'
> Ni uuas noh than thiu tid cuman (*Heliand* 852)
> 'the time had not yet come'
> ða hine Wedera cyn
> for herebrogan habban ni mihte (*Beowulf* 461-62)
> 'when the tribe of the Weders would not have him for dread of battle'
> ic hine ne mihte...
> ganges getwæman (*Beowulf* 967-68)
> 'I could not prevent him from going'

In Old English the negative particle is often compounded with the verb if the verb is light, e.g., *nolde* 'did not want', *næs* 'was not', etc.

In the West Germanic dialects, then, the negation and the finite verb form a close syntactic unit which are not separable from one another. In Gothic, too, the negative particle in qualitative negation is placed immediately before the finite verb, but particles and adverbs closely associated with the verb may intervene between the negation and the verb.

> ni balwjais mis
> μή με βασανίσῃς
> 'do not torment me' (*Mark* 5, 7)

But:

> ni-u andhafjis waiht?
> οὐκ ἀποκρίνῃ οὐδεν
> 'do you not answer?' (*Mark* 14, 60)

In the West Germanic dialects quantitative negation is often accompanied by a repetition of the negative particle before the verb, as in the following examples:

> 7 þa cudedon hie þæt him nænig mæg leofra nære þonne
> hiera hlaford (*Chronicle* 755 A.D.)
> 'and they said that no one could be dearer to them than their lord'
> þæt hie nænig mon siþþan findan ne meahte (*Chronicle* 418 A.D.)
> 'that afterwards no one could find them'

[2]   V. E. Mourek, *Zur Negation im Altgermanischen* (Prague, Verlag der Kgl. Böhmischen Gesellschaft der Wissenschaften, 1903).
[3]   Delbrück, *Syntax I.*
[4]   Mourek, *Negation*, p. 2, fn. 2.

Yet in Gothic no such repetition was necessary; we find, for example, *ni manna mag twaim fraujam skalkinon* οὐδεὶς δύναται δύσι κυρίοις δουλεύειν 'no man may serve two masters' (*Matthew* 6, 24) and not **ni manna ni mag* (cf. Old English *nænig ne meahte*). In Gothic *ni* could be placed either before a noun phrase (quantitative negation) or before a verb (qualitative negation). In some respects *ni* in Gothic resembles syntactically the preverbs. Like the preverbs, *ni* can be followed by enclitic particles, as in *ni-u andhafjis* (above), and *nih* 'nec' (cf. also *niþ-þan mag* οὐ δύναται δε 'for he cannot' [*Corinthians* I, 12, 21] beside *at-uh-þan-gaf* δεδώκει δε 'then he gave' [*Mark* 14, 44]). If the verb is modified by a preverb, *ni* often intervenes between the preverb and the verb, e.g., *miþ-ni-qam* οὐ συνεισῆλθεν 'did not go in' (*John* 6, 22), *inn-ni-atgaggiþ* μη εἰσερχόμενος 'does not go in' (*John* 10, 1). In Old English we find a similar pattern in *on ne gedyde* 'did not do on' (*Chronicle* 81 A.D.). Although the Gothic evidence is not consistent (cf. for example *ni-miþ-matjan* 'not to eat with' *Corithians* I, 5, 11), the patterns which I have described for Gothic accord with the comparative syntax of the negative particle. In Hittite also, enclitic particles may be attached to a negation, and the negative particle may be placed between the preverb and the verb. According to Friedrich: "The usual position of the negation is before the verb form, with compound verbs between preverb and verb form."[5] We find, for the compound verb: ᵁᴿᵁ*Ha-ak-pis-sa-an-mu-kan... arha U-UL da-a-as* 'But he did not take away from me Hakpissas' (*Hattusilis* 11), and for the simple verb: *nu-us-ma-as I-NA MU 10 KAM S(E) NU-MUN U-UL an-ni-es-ki-ir* 'they did not plant seed there for ten years' (*Hattusilis* 6); and with enclitics: *U-UL-as-mu me-na-ah-ha-an-da mar-ah-ta* 'he did not succeed against me' (*Hattusilis* 11).

3. *The 'Preverb'*

In all of the Indo-European languages the immediate lexical meaning of the verb could be extended by the combination of the verb with a particle known as a preverb. In the erliest dialects the preverb is not a verbal prefix, as it often later became, but is freely detachable from the verb and could appear, after the fashion of an adverb, in almost any position in the clause. Two of these positions are assumed by Watkins[6] to be basic, the contact position and the position at the head of the clause, symbolized as follows:

$$\#... \, PV\#$$
$$\#P... \, V\#$$

Vedic examples illustrate this situation.

> tam cid eva api gacchatāt (*RV* X, 154, 2)
> 'those (two) shall join them'
> apa tye tāyave yathā naksatrā yanti (*RV* I, 50, 3)
> 'away those stars like robbers go'

5 Johannes Friedrich, *Hethitisches Elementarbuch*, 2nd ed. (Heidelberg, Winter, 1960), p. 147.
6 Watkins, "Sentence Structure":1041-42.

The accentuation of preverb and verb in Sanskrit suggests that the two formed a syntactic unit of some kind. The pattern was for the preverb to be accented in main clauses and the verb unaccented, e.g., *prá gacchati* 'he goes forth'. But in subordinate clauses, the verb received the accent and the preverb lost its accent when in contact: *yáḥ pra gácchati* 'who goes forth'.

When a preverb appeared with a transitive verb having an object noun, structural ambiguity could arise, for the 'preverb' was capable of interpretation either as an 'adverb' in construction with the verb, or as a postposition governing the object noun (the complex of postposition and noun being now interpreted as a postpositional phrase complementary to the verb). This phenomenon is discussed by Delbrück,[7] with examples from Sanskrit such as *ati tṛṣṭam vavakṣita* 'du bist über das Beissende (den Rauch) emporgestiegen' (*RV* III, 9, 3) with tmesis (separation of preverb and verb), and *dasvasam upa gacchatam* 'kommt zum Verehrer, besucht den Verehrer' (*RV* I, 47, 3) for the contact position.

In so far as it was a type of directional complement,[8] the preverb in Germanic could appear at a point widely separated from the verb. In Old English, for example, it may be placed before a prepositional phrase, to which it may be in a kind of appositional relationship:

> ær hie ut of þam geweore foron (*Chronicle* 896 A.D.)
> 'before they moved out of the fortification'

After the verb:

> 7 þa foron þa men ut ongean (*Chronicle* 921 A.D.)
> 'and the men moved out again'

Or in the 'classic' preverb position, before a final verb:

> swa þa oþra hergas mid ealle herige ut foron (*Chronicle* 894 A.D.)
> 'as soon as the other armies moved out in full force'
> þæt hie gesunde from eodon (*Chronicle* 755 A.D.)
> 'that they got away safe and sound'

This latter, contact, position is most frequently found with the final verb.

A postpositional use of the preverb is found in all dialects. In West Germanic it is largely, perhaps exclusively, restricted to pronouns.

> 7 þa Francan him wiþ fuhton (*Chronicle* 881 A.D.)
> 'and the Franks fought against him'
>   (daz frono chruci)
> dar der heligo Crist ana arhangan uuard (*Muspilli*, 100-01)
> '(The holy cross) on which the blessed Christ was hanged'
> 7 þære rode dæl þe Crist on þrowude (*Chronicle* 885 A.D.)
> 'and a portion of the cross on which Christ suffered'
> þæt he þone dæg forlure þe he noht to gode on ne gedyde (*Chronicle* 81 A.D.)
> 'that that day was lost to him on which he did no good'

[7] Delbrück, *Vergleichende Syntax*, vol. I, 654-57.
[8] See pp. 73-74.

But in Old Norse no such restriction exists. Heusler's discussion shows such postpositions to be common with respect to pronouns and particles (especially relatives):

> verþet, þat er Bolle hefer mer fyrer heitet landet[9]
> 'the amount which Bolle had promised me for the land'

and, mainly in poetic usage, with nouns, as in the following example:

> Ut þu ne komir orom hollom fra,
> nema þu inn snotrari ser (*Vafðrúðnismál* 7)[10]
> 'You shall not leave our hall unless you are the cleverer'

The syntax of the preverbs is one of the more puzzling aspects of Indo-European and Germanic grammar, but a few hazardous generalizations may be made. It seems that actual prefixation with the verb is a relatively late device. In Gothic, for example, enclitics may intervene even between the 'aspectual' preverb *ga-* and the verb, e.g., *ga-u-hwa-sehwi*. The preverb was either a (directional) adverb or a postposition, and the distinction between the two functions may always have been a fluid one in some cases. The postpositional syntagm survived longest when pronouns and particles were involved; in this respect we may compare the similar situation in Latin, where the combinations *mecum*, etc., are preserved into classical times, although postpositions with nouns are found in the oldest period of the language and the Italic dialects.[11] Tmesis appears to be a special case of fronting of emphatic adverbs, so that the clause initial 'preverbs' often found in Germanic alliterative verse are comparable to the basic Indo-European syntagms described by Watkins and mentioned above. Examples are:

> (Ic eom frod feores,) fram ic ne wille, (*Battle of Maldon*, l. 317)
> 'I am old in years; I will not leave (the battle)'

> (eoletes æt ende). þanon up hraðe
> Wedera leode on wang stigon (*Beowulf* 224-25)
> '(after the dismounting). From there the tribe of the Weders stepped up on to dry land'

> (fet ond folma). Forþ near ætstop (*Beowulf* 745)
> '(hand and foot). He stepped forward nearer'

> Ut þu ne komir orom hollom fra (*Vafðrúðnismal* 7)[12]
> 'You shall not leave our halls'

The position immediately before the verb was fundamental, and is almost invariable when the verb is final. Delbrück has pointed out that in Gothic preverbs such as *inn* are placed before the verb in subordinate clauses, e.g.:[13]

> sæi inn ni atgaggiþ
> 'who does not enter in'
> ὁ μὴ εἰσερχόμενος (*John* 10, 1)

---

9 Heusler, *Elementarbuch*, p. 145.
10 From Neckel, *Edda*.
11 J. B. Hofmann, *Lateinische Syntax und Stylistik*, neubear. v. Anton Szantyr (München, Beck, 1965) vol. II, p. 215.
12 From Neckel, *Edda*.
13 Berthold Delbrück, "Zur Stellung des Verbums im Gotischen und Altindischen", *PBB* 36 (1910): 359-62.

In the Nordic languages the preverb often precedes a final non-finite verb, as in the following examples from Old Swedish

> gangær at stiæla bryti ok þræl, bryti skal uppi hængia[14]
> 'Geht stehlen ein Aufseher und ein Knecht, der Aufseher soll hangen'

and Old Norse:

> at han skylde log þeira upp segia (*Libellus Islandorum*)[15]
> 'that he should expound their law'

The syntax of the 'preverbs' in Germanic, then, has archaic characteristics with parallels in the oldest Indo-European dialects. The two basic positions, that immediately preceding the final verb, and that at the head of a clause, are found in Germanic, and the syntagm PREVERB — VERB with final verb was probably the fundamental one. The placing of enclitics between a preverb and verb found in Gothic may be compared with similar patterns in Hittite and Old Irish described by Dillon:[15]

> Hittite: *para-(a)n-pesta* 'he gave him away'
> Old Irish: *da-m-beir* 'he brings him'
> Gothic: *at-uh-þan gaf* 'and he gave'
> *ga-u-hwa sehwi* 'whether he saw anything'

These patterns show that the 'inseparable prefixes' of the Germanic dialects are a relatively late development. Proto-Germanic was exclusively a suffixing language. The development of prepositions and verbal prefixes out of postpositions and directional adverbs is in line with the general typological shift from *SOV* (SUBJECT-OBJECT-VERB) to *SVO* constituent ordering

If the syntactic resemblances between Germanic and other early Indo-European dialects with respect to the preverb are close, the same cannot be said of the accentuation. The Germanic 'adverbial' preverb was (and in the modern dialects still is) more heavily stressed than the verb; in poetry it often alliterates. In Sanskrit the main clause preverb is accented. Bonfante has claimed [16] to have discerned in Germanic the same accentual contrast between a main and a subordinate clause verb as existed in Sanskrit, an accented preverb and unaccented verb in the main clause, and an unaccented preverb and accented verb in the subordinate clause. Unfortunately, Bonfante bases his conclusions on a brief examination of the written accents in Otfrid von Weissenburg's *Evangelienbuch*. Not only is there much uncertainty about the nature of these accents, but even a glance at a different section of the *Evangelienbuch* from that examined by Bonfante reveals no consistency in the accentuation of preverb and verb in main and subordinate clauses. At least the adverbial type of preverb, then, did not form a close syntactic unit with the verb, as it did in Sanskrit.

---

[14] Berthold Delbrück, *Germanische Syntax IV: Die Wortstellung in dem älteren westgötischen Landrecht* (Leipzig, Teubner, 1918), p. 15.
[15] E. V. Gordon, *An Introduction to Old Norse*, 2nd ed., A. R. Taylor, rev. (Oxford, Clarendon Press, 1957), p. 37.
[16] Bonfante, "Proposizione":41-47.

4. *The Non-Finite Verb*

In all the early Germanic dialects the non-finite verb was placed toward the end of the clause. It was often in the final position when the finite verb was in second place, or was followed only by adverbial elements. If the finite verb itself was at the end of the clause with the non-finite verb, the two elements show in the recorded dialects some variation in their relative ordering. The ordering VERB — AUXILIARY probably predominates, however. If the Germanic dental preterite is in fact an original auxiliary from *dhē- (and, despite the many differences of opinion on this point, forms such as Gothic *tawidedun* will probably always make this an attractive interpretation), then the order VERB — AUXILIARY is confirmed. The following examples are representative of the situation in the dialects, with both orderings illustrated:

> 7 se here þa burg be seten hæfde (*Chronicle* 894 A.D.)
> 'and the Danish army had occupied the city'
>
> þæt hi hine ne mehton ferian (*Chronicle* 894 A.D.)
> 'that they could not take him with them'
>
> 7 hie hindan ofridan ne meahte (*Chronicle* 877 A.D.)
> 'and was not able to catch up with them'
>
> ef gi im thus fulgangan uuillead (*Heliand* 1689)
> 'if you thus take thought for him'
>
>   er it im the helago Crist
> obar that erlo folc ...
> ...   seggean uuelda (*Heliand* 2372-74)
> 'before holy Christ wished to tell it to the good people'
>
>   that he sie gerno forð
> lestien uuillie (*Heliand* 2498-99)
> 'that he might want to carry out (the words)'
>
> so dar manno nohhein uuiht pimidan ni mak (*Muspilli* 90)
> 'Thus no man there can in any way avoid it'
>
> en þa es hann hafþe her veret einn vetr eþa tua (*Libellus Islandorum*)[17]
> 'but when he had been there one or two winters'
>
> at hann skylde log þeira upp segia (*Libellus Islandorum*)[18]
> 'that he should expound their law'

If the non-finite verb is a verb of motion, it is often omitted, as in the following two examples from Old English:

> þær him mon to ne meahte (*Chronicle* 877 A.D.)
> 'where no one could get to him'
>
> þa þe him from noldon (*Chronicle* 755, A.D.)
> 'those who did not want to leave him'

B. SECTION II: THE SYNTAX OF THE FINITE VERB

Earlier investigations of Indo-European verbal syntax proposed three basic positions for the finite verb. Two of these are described by Delbrück: "The verb in the indepen-

---

[17]   Gordon, *Old Norse*, p. 36.
[18]   Gordon, *Old Norse*, p. 37.

dent statement clause stood at the end and was weakly accented. If it was especially important, it came at the head of the clause and was strongly accented."[19] Wackernagel had already suggested that the verb could also appear in the enclitic, or clause-second, position under some circumstances. In Sanskrit the verb of a main clause was unaccented, while that of a subordinate clause was accented. It was improbable, Wackernagel argued, that the proto-language could have had such an accentual contrast without also having had a positional contrast.[20] He therefore concluded that in the Proto-Indo-European main clause the verb stood in the enclitic position, and the verb of the subordinate clause was placed at the end of the clause. Delbrück also later admitted the possibility of the finite verb in the enclitic position.[21]

Any of these positions could be modified in certain ways. Unaccented sentence-initial particles could be disregarded, so that an immediately following accented element could still be followed by an enclitic verb. Explanatory or amplifying elements, which were not essential to the structure of the clause, could be added after a clause-final verb.

In addition to positing these three fundamental places of the verb in the Proto-Indo-European sentence, scholars also hypothesized the conditions under which the one or the other was used. According to Wackernagel, the enclitic verb was characteristic of main clauses; Wackernagel, however, placed the following limitation on the sentence-second position of the main clause verb. He assumed:

that the monosyllabic or disyllabic verb forms, and the shorter verb forms in general, shifted to a certain extent to the second position, but that on the other hand the other verb forms had the subordinate clause position even in main clauses.[22]

In a main clause, therefore, the place of the verb depended on what it is convenient to call the "weight"[23] of the verb, its length in syllables. The long and short verbs were syntactically in complementary distribution, such that the long ('heavy') verbs were placed at the end of the clause, the short ('light') ones were attracted into the enclitic position. We may therefore treat the enclitic and final verb of the main clause as variants of the same positional feature. The circumstances under which the clause-final verb occurred were probably similar to those described for Sanskrit by Gonda: "When the verb terminates the clause, the style is unified, narrative and communicative."[24] In the older Slavic languages, too, although vivid narration is characterized by clause-initial verbs, the final position of the verb is used for narrative description

---

19   Delbrück, *Vergleichende Syntax*, vol. I, p. 83.
20   Wackernagel, "Über ein Gesetz":427.
21   Delbrück, *Germanische Syntax II*, pp. 65-76.
22   Wackernagel, "Über ein Gesetz":427.
23   The term corresponds to the German *Körperlichkeit* as used by Ries, Kuhn and other scholars. Cf. also Fourquet's adoption of *léger* and *lourd* from Ries' *leicht* and *schwer* (Fourquet, *L'ordre*, p. 13.
24   Jan Gonda, *Remarques sur la place du verbe dans la phrase active et moyenne en langue sanscrite* (Utrecht, A. Oosthoek, 1953), p. 40.

and commentary.[25] The sentence-final position, then, was typical of neutral, unemphatic sentences; it was the normal or 'unmarked' position of the finite verb.

The Indo-European situation in which a neutral sentence type with final verb existed, but in which other positions of the verb were also possible raises a number of questions concerning the 'syntactic typology' of Proto-Indo-European. According to Greenberg,[26] a 'verb-final', or *SOV*, language should show a number of concomitant phenomena such as postpositions rather than prepositions, preposed relative clauses, the standard preceding the comparative adjective, the adnominal genitive preceding the head noun, etc. Traces of all of these phenomena are in fact recoverable from the early Indo-European dialects, and significantly they become more numerous the further back one goes in time; for example, postpositions are frequent in Early Latin and the other Italic dialects, but are rare in Classical Latin; the gradual shift from a predominant order GENITIVE — NOUN to a predominant order NOUN — GENITIVE is traced in an article by Rosenkranz;[27] and verb-final sentences are preponderant in the earliest Latin texts. Somewhat similar observations may be made concerning Sanskrit, Hittite and Germanic (but not concerning Greek).

Yet there is some unwillingness to accept a basic order with final verb for the early Indo-European dialects and Proto-Indo-European. Basing his conclusions on the behavior of "gapping rules", Ross has claimed that all of the Indo-European languages have or had the underlying order *SVO*.[28] And Lakoff, in her study of Latin complementation, defends the view that in Latin, too, the underlying order is that in which objects follow the verb.[29] McCawley suggests, like Ross, that in 'true' *SOV* languages no compromise is possible with respect to the absolute final position of the verb; a language in which the verb is able to be shifted out of the final position cannot be a 'true' *SOV* language.[30]

Nonetheless, the typological criteria developed by Greenberg, when applied to early Indo-European, point to *SOV* word order. Gonda's studies of Sanskrit show that the final verb reflected a stylistically neutral sentence-type,[31] and I shall show that the evidence of the early Germanic dialects indicates a similar situation in Proto-Germanic. The 'gapping' hypothesis, that in *SOV* languages common elements are deleted from left to right, is not itself 'evidence' of a true *SOV* language, but only of the hypothesis that such languages have only verb-final sentences. In Latin, for example, gapping is left to right when the verb is final:

25   Berneker, in Delbrück, *Vergleichende Syntax*, vol. III, p. 73.
26   Greenberg, *Universals*.
27   B. Rosenkranz, "Die Stellung des attributiven Genetivs im Italischen", *IF* 51 (1933):131-39.
28   J. R. Ross, "Gapping and the Order of Constituents" in *Progress in Linguistics*, M. Bierswisch and K. E. Heidolph, eds. (The Hague, Mouton, 1970), pp. 249-59. *Gapping* is the deletion of one instance of the same verb occurring in conjoined sentences, as in "Hans ordered beer and Fritz wine".
29   R. Lakoff, *Abstract Syntax*, pp. 100-01.
30   J. McCawley, "English as a *VSO* Language", *Language* 46 (1970). 2 (Part I):286-99.
31   Gonda, *Remarques*.

ipsorum lingua Celtae, nostra Galli appellantur (Ceasar, *De Bello Gallico* I, 1,1,
cit., Marouzeau, p. 14)
'in their own tongue they are called Celts, in ours, Gauls'

and in other sentence-types from right to left:

Vicit pudorem libido, timorem audacia, rationem amentia (Cicero, *Pro Cluento* 15,
cit. Marouzeau, p. 45)
'lust overcomes modesty, rashness fear, frenzy reason'

A similar phenomenon in German is described by Ross.[32] Hence the direction of
gapping cannot be used as evidence that all Indo-European languages, and also
Proto-Indo-European, are or were *SVO* languages. At the most, if the data are correct,
it could show that in none of the modern dialects is the final position the sole possible
one for the verb. It does not alter the fact that the oldest layers of Indo-European show
a predominantly *SOV* surface word order, still less suggest how this is to be accounted
for unless Proto-Indo-European is assumed to be of the *SOV* type.

Proto-Germanic also had a neutral, unmarked sentence-type with final verb, an
alternative to which was the enclitic verb if the verb was 'light'. We also find evidence
of marked or emphatic sentence-types with initial verbs. However, a change was
taking place the effects of which may be seen in the earliest written monuments of the
Germanic languages. The sentence-second or enclitic position was becoming genera-
lized at the expense of the final and initial positions. The reason for this change was
probably the increase in the number of light verbs which resulted from the growing
tendency to express tense and mood by means of an auxiliary verb rather than by verbal inflection.[33] There is also evidence that the enclitic verb often shared the positional characteristics of the particles and pronouns in appearing towards the beginning
of the sentence, or even at the head of the sentence, in proclisis to the first autonomous
element. In alliterative verse, for example, a light verb is frequently in anacrusis, together with particles and pronouns, in the unaccented onset syllables preceding the first
alliterating syllable in the line. If the verb is initial and does not alliterate, it is presumably sometimes a reflex of an enclitic rather than an originally sentence-initial verb.

Just as a clause-initial verb in Germanic does not necessarily reflect a Proto-Indo-
European clause-initial verb, so do we find sentence-second verbs which reflect, not an
earlier neutral order, but a marked order. Unaccented particles may precede the verb
and be in proclisis to it; indeed, the syntagm PARTICLE + VERB was perhaps more
frequent than the unmodified initial verb in sequence-initial clauses. As Delbrück
recognized, a verb preceded by a particle is not always in enclisis to the particle, but
may be in modified or "covered" (*gedeckt*) initial position.[34]

---

[32] Ross, "Gapping".
[33] Cf. Delbrück, *Germanische Syntax II*, p. 15.
[34] Delbrück, *Vergleichende Syntax*, vol. III, 67.

1. *Part I: The Proto-Indo-European Clause-Initial Verb in Germanic*

a. *Specialized Functions of the Clause-Initial Verb*

(1) *Imperatives*

There is perhaps no grammatical construction in which the emphasis is as clearly on the verbal idea as in the imperative. It is therefore to be expected that imperative clauses in Proto-Indo-European and Proto-Germanic should have the verb in the initial position. According to Gonda, the imperative is one of the constructions in Sanskrit in which the verb is found at the head of the clause. In Germanic, although the imperative does not always alliterate, it is usually placed at the head of the clause, and is stressed more often than the normal finite verb, as in the following examples:

> Geþenc nu, se mæra maga Healfdenes (*Beowulf* 1474)
> 'Remember now, great son of Healfdene'
>
> Ne sorga, snotor guma (*Beowulf* 1384)
> 'Don't worry, wise man'
>
> Aris, rices weard (*Beowulf* 1390)
> 'Arise, guardian of the realm'

Meillet has drawn attention to a feature of word-order in Gothic imperative clauses.[35] Occurrences of the Greek form καθαρίσθητι are invariably rendered *wairþ hrains* 'be pure', whereas the word-order of the indicative ἐκαθαρίσθη 'was purified' is *hrains warp*.

The imperative could, however, stand at the end of the clause under specified conditions; this phenomenon is discussed by Andrew in *Syntax and Style in Old English*,[36] and examples are also found in other Germanic dialects. If more than one imperative occurs consecutively in the same unified series of sentences, only the first imperative clause has the initial verb; subsequent imperatives, as shown in the following examples, have a final verb:

> Bruc þisses beages, Beowulf leofa,
> hyse, mid hæle, ond þisses hrægles neot (*Beowulf* 1216-17)
> 'Wear this necklace, dear Beowulf, with prosperity, and enjoy this mantle'
>
> Onfoh þissum fulle, freodrihten min,
> sinces brytta! þu on sælum wes,
> goldwine gumena, ond to Geatum spræc
> mildum wordum (*Beowulf* 1169-70)
> 'Accept this cup, my beloved lord, giver of treasure; be happy, gold-friend of men, and speak to the Goths with kind words'
>
> Ga nu to setle, symbelwynne dreoh (*Beowulf* 1782)
> 'Go now to your seat, enjoy the feast'
>
> Bebeorh þe ðonne bealonið, Beowulf leofa,
> secg besta, ond þe þæt selre geceos,
> ece rædas; oferhyda ne gym,
> mære cempa! (*Beowulf* 1758-61)

---

[35] Meillet, "Faits gothiques":97.
[36] S. O. Andrew, *Syntax and Style in Old English* (Cambridge, Cambridge University Press, 1940), p. 68.

'Be on your guard against evil, dear Beowulf, best of warriors, and choose for yourself the better, eternal counsels. Do not heed arrogance, greatest of champions'

ne beo þu ne forht, ne on mode ne murn (*Andreas* 98)
'Do not be afraid, or worry in your mind'

Ni brutti thih muates, noh thines anluzzes
farauua ni uuenti: fol bistu gotes ensti! (*Otfrid*, I, 5, 17-18)
'Do not be startled in your mind, nor change the colour of your face: you are full of God's grace!'[37]

than nim thu ina sundar te thi,
thene rink an runa endi imu is rad saga (*Heliand* 3225-26)
'then take him aside and secretly give him this advice'

Fourquet finds the word order of the following Gothic imperative surprising[38]: *Zakkaiu, sniumands dalaþ atsteig* Ζακχαῖε σπεύσας κατάβηθι, 'Zakkaius, hurry! climb down!' (*Luke* 19, 5,); yet if we construe the participial form *sniumands* semantically as an imperative, *atsteig* can be regarded as a 'serial' imperative whose word-order agrees with that of the same construction in other Germanic dialects.

Hirt describes a similar phenomenon in Greek,[39] with the examples:

ψεύδη δὲ μηδέν, ἀλλὰ πάντα τ' ἀλῆθη λέγε (*Lysias* 1, 18)
'don't lie, but tell the whole truth'

χαίρετε, κήρυκες, ἆσσον ἴτε (*Iliad* I, 334)
'greetings, you heralds; come closer'

In Sanskrit, consecutive imperatives are occasionally accented even when in the final position, i.e., the consecutive imperative behaves like a dependent clause: *tū́yam ā́ gahi kā́ṇveṣu sú sácā píba* 'come hither quickly; drink along with the Kanvas.'[40] I shall show that in Proto-Germanic the final verb was normal in sentences forming part of a series (intra-sequential sentences). The syntax of the imperative is further evidence that in Proto-Indo-European also the verb was usually final in intra-sequential clauses.

(2) Yes-No Questions

Yes-no questions in Proto-Indo-European were constructed by uttering the simple statement with special intonation.[41] If a particular word was to be interrogated, that word was placed at the head of the clause, and could be emphasized by attaching to it an enclitic particle. If no particular word, but the whole clause was to be interrogated, the verb was placed in the head position, i.e., the sentence had the marked word-order; again, the verb could be emphasized by an enclitic particle. Particles could become specialized in their function of emphasizing a word to be interrogated, and themselves become the performer of the interrogative function; thus Gothic *u*, interrogative particle, beside Sanskrit *u*, emphatic particle.

---

[37] See p. 23, for the primary sources of Otfrid and *Andreas*.
[38] Fourquet, *L'ordre*, p. 269.
[39] Hirt, *Grammatik*, vol. VII, p. 255.
[40] Whitney, *Sanskrit*, p. 225 (paragraph 595d); Delbrück, *Vergleichende Syntax*, vol. III, p. 418.
[41] Cf. Hirt, *Grammatik*, vol. VII, pp. 35-41.

Gothic is the only Germanic dialect which retains more than vestiges of an interrogative particle. Since the word-order of the Gothic documents is Greek rather than Germanic, we can make no useful statement about the frequency of the sentence-initial verb in yes-no questions. The only syntactic statement possible is that if the verb was compounded with a preverb, the interrogative particle usually intervened between the preverb and the verb, as for example *ga-u-laubjats* 'do you believe?' (*Matthew* 9, 28). Fourquet assumes that "when the question does not bear upon a determined constituent of the clause, the enclitic *u* is attached to the verb. This group is always at the head of the clause."[42] The only citable examples, however, are in indirect questions:

> þankeiþ, siai-u mahteigs
> βουλεύεται εἰ δυνατός ἐστιν (*Luke* 14, 31)
> 'he considers whether he is able'
>
> jah witaidedun imma, hailidedi-u sabbato daga
> και παρετηροῦντο αὐτόν, εἰ τοῖς σαββασιν θεραπεύσει αὐτόν (*Mark* 3, 2)
> 'they watched him, whether he would heal on the Sabbath'

In the other Germanic dialects there is ample evidence of interrogative clauses with initial verb, so that the construction may safely be assumed for Proto-Germanic, presumably together with constructions involving interrogative particles. Examples are:

> Eart þu se Beowulf se þe wið Brecan wunne? (*Beowulf* 506)
> 'Are you that Beowulf who strove with Breca?'
>
> bist thu than thoh Helias? (*Heliand* 920)
> 'Are you then perhaps Elias?'
>
> scal ik im sibun siðun iro sundea aletan? (*Heliand* 3245)
> 'shall I forgive them their sins seven times?'

(3) *Conditional Sentences*

The type of conditional sentence in which the verb of the prior clause is at the head of the clause was probably Proto-Germanic. Numerous examples are found in the Old Swedish land laws, many of which are formulated in the manner:

> hængir klocka i kirkiu, faldær i hovod mannæ, böti sopn firi[43]
> 'if a bell hangs in a church, and it falls on someone's head, let the parish pay'

Behaghel assumed that the construction originated from a question-and-answer syntagm, in which the prior clause posed a hypothetical question and the posterior clause gave an answer.[44] Hirt supported this explanation, and suggested that the construction was Proto-Indo-European, and antedated the use of particles such as 'if'.[45]

---

[42]   Fourquet, *L'ordre*, p. 255.
[43]   Delbrück, *Germanische Syntax IV*, p. 14.
[44]   Otto Behaghel, *Deutsche Syntax, eine geschichtliche Darstellung* (Heidelberg, Winter, 1928), vol. III, p. 637.
[45]   Hirt, *Handbuch*, vol. III, p. 205.

Behaghel's explanation was presumably based on the notion that only special sentence-types could have the initial verb, such as questions and imperatives. In Proto-Germanic, however, the clause-initial verb was a possible emphatic alternative to the final and enclitic verb. I therefore regard the word-order of conditional sentences as the normal emphatic word-order, and the clauses of the condition as a series of statements such that the prior ones describe a situation and the posterior ones draw a conclusion from it. There is then no difficulty in explaining the occasional inconsistencies found in which one or all of the clauses of the conditional series do not have the initial verb, e.g.:

> farr annar broþer köpferþum ok annar hemæ i asku sitær,
> baþir eighu þer iammykit af arvi[46]
> 'if one brother goes off on a commercial venture and the other sits at home by the hearth, both shall have an equal share of the inheritance'

(4) Negative Clauses

In Gothic the verb *wairþan*, when negated, is often followed by its predicate without any precedent from the *Vorlage*, e.g.,

> ni wairþiþ garaihts manna
> οὐ δικαιοῦται ἄνθρωπος
> 'man is not justified' (*Galatians* 2, 16)

Meillet has compared this special syntactic feature of the negated verb with the special accentuation of the verb *to be* in Armenian and Greek. In Greek ἐστὶ is normally an enclitic, but when preceded by certain particles, among them οὐκ, it receives a full accent: οὐκ ἔστι.[47]

In other Germanic dialects also, the initial position of a negated verb is frequent. According to Schuchardt,[48] the verbs in *Beowulf* which are negated with *ne* occur at the head of the clause 79 times, and elsewhere in the clause 109 times. In view of the comparatively low frequency of clause-initial verbs, this high incidence of negated verbs in the initial position is significant. In the *Heliand*, too, negated clauses are often introduced by the verb, although no statistics are available. In Modern English *to be* is less commonly enclitic when negated, e.g., *John's a bore* but, in a neutral context, *John isn't a bore* rather than *John's not a bore*; furthermore, the negated full verb is subject to the periphrastic *do* construction, which corresponds syntactically to the emphatic verb of early Germanic dialects.

b. *Non-Specialized Functions of the Clause-Initial Verb*

Not only special sentence-types such as questions and imperatives, but also statements could under some circumstances have the finite verb in the head position. Such

---

[46] Delbrück, *Germanische Syntax IV*, p. 16.
[47] Meillet, "Faits gothiques":97-98.
[48] Richard Schuchardt, *Die Negation im Beowulf* (Berlin, Ebering, 1910), pp. 22-31.

statements were emphatic or dramatic, or they stood outside a sequence of clauses, or they introduced a sequence of clauses. In Germanic poetry the initial verb is frequent; in prose it is more often reflected in the use of a sequence-introducing proclitic particle, especially *þa*, followed immediately by the verb. The greater frequency of the initial verb in poetry is probably a result of the poet's inclination for dramatic effects, but could also represent an archaizing tendency in alliterative verse. In the *Chronicle* the syntagm *þa* + VERB regularly introduces a new development in a narrative:

Her to dælde se fore sprecena here on tu...; 7 ymb sæton þa ceastre, 7 worhton oþer fæsten ymb hie selfe. 7 hie þeah þa ceastre aweredon oþþæt Ælfred com utan mid fierde. *Ia eode* se here to hiera scipum, 7 forlet þæt geworc... (*Chronicle* 885 A.D.)

'In this year the previously mentioned [Danish] army divided into two parts...and besieged the town, and they built another fortification around themselves. The citizens, however, defended themselves until King Alfred came to them with auxiliaries. Then the [Danish] army went to their ships, and deserted their fortifications'

In *Beowulf* and the *Heliand* the verb is often found in the initial position in lively narrative sequences and in sequence-initial sentences. In the following example from *Beowulf*, a sequence is brought to an end by the warriors' launching of the boat, and a new one is initiated by the description of the moving boat:

> guman ut scufon
> weras on wilsið wudu bundenne.
> Gewat þa ofer wægholm winde gefysed
> flota famiheals fugle gelicost (*Beowulf* 215-18)

'the men — warriors on a longed-for voyage — pushed out the bound planks. Then, over the breaking sea, driven by the wind, the boat departed, like a bird, its neck foam-flecked'

Often, as here, such initial verbs alliterate (finite verbs do not otherwise normally alliterate in Germanic verse). The accentuation of the initial verb is presumably inherited from Proto-Indo-European; in Sanskrit the clause-initial verb is also accented.[49]

2. *Part II*: *The Proto-Indo-European Clause-Final and Enclitic Verb in Proto-Germanic*

a. *The Final Verb*

In his analysis of Sanskrit verbal syntax, Gonda describes the conditions under which the finite verb is placed at the end of its clause:[50] "When the verb terminates the clause, the style is unified, narrative and communicative." In the earliest Germanic monuments the verb in the unmarked clause already shows a tendency to occupy the second, originally enclitic, position. The earlier, Proto-Germanic, situation, in which the neutral verb is clause-final unless it is light, survives especially in extended sequences of sentences in narrative style. Most of the major narrative passages in the *Chronicle* provide several examples; I give two such passages:

49   Whitney, *Sanskrit*, p. 223 (paragraph 592).
50   Gonda, *Remarques*, p. 40.

7 hie late on geare to þam gecirdon þæt hi wiþ þonne here winnende wærun, 7 hie þeah micle fierd gegadrodon, 7 þone here sohton æt Eoforwic ceastre, 7 on þa ceastre bræcon, 7 hie sume inne wurdon, 7 þær was ungemetlic wæl geslægen Norþan hymbra, sume binnan, sume butan; 7 þa cyninges begen ofslægene, 7 sio laf wiþ þonne here friþ nam. (*Chronicle* 867 A.D.)

'And late in the year they made preparation to engage the [Danish] army, and they gathered a large body of militia and sought out the Danish army at York, and stormed the city, and some got inside, and there was great slaughter of the Northumbrians, some within and some without; the two kings were slain, and the survivors made peace with the Danes'

7 þa geascode he þone cyning lytle werode on wyf cyþþe on Meran tune, 7 hine þær berad, 7 þone bur utan be eode ær hine þa men onfunden þe mid þæm cyninge wærun; 7 þa ongeat se cyning þæt, 7 he on þa duru eode, 7 þa unheanlice hine werede, oþ he on þone æþelinge locude, 7 þa utræsde on hine, 7 hine miclum gewundode, 7 hie alle on þone cyning feohtende wæron oþ þæt hie hine ofslægenne hæfdon... (*Chronicle* 755 A.D.)

'And then he found out that the king was visiting a mistress with a small retinue in Meranton; and he surprised him there, and surrounded the hut before the men who were with the king were aware of it. And then the king perceived this, and went to the door and gallantly defended himself until he saw the prince. Then he rushed out on him and severely wounded him, and they all fell upon the king until they had slain him'

In such narrative sequences the pattern of the verb position is typically:

Initial sentence: $\#þa$ + Verb...
Subsequent sentences: $\#7$ ... Verb$\#$

I here make a distinction between SEQUENTIAL, or INTRA-SEQUENTIAL, and EXTRA-SEQUENTIAL clauses. The distinction resembles in part that made by Kuhn between independent (*selbständig*) and bound (*gebunden*) clauses.[51] According to Kuhn, who based his views principally on the oldest Norse poetry, the *dróttkvaett* verse, the verb in Proto-Germanic was initial in independent, final in bound clauses; Kuhn wrote: "I am concerned to prove that a difference in the position of the verb in independent and bound clauses, similar to that which exists in New High German between main and subordinate clauses, once existed in all Germanic dialects."[52] There is a difference between my SEQUENTIAL and Kuhn's "bound" clause, in that bound clauses are those "which are arranged in series with another clause by means of a conjunction",[53] whereas in my analysis the deciding factor is not the introductory particle but the position of the whole clause. If, for example, Old English *ond* is frequently accompanied by a final verb, it is because *ond* always introduces an interior clause, and not because of syntactic quality of the particle itself.[54] Similarly the particle *þa* is usually followed by a verb in (covered) initial position; but if, as in the following passage, *þa* introduces a clause regarded as belonging to the same narrative series as the preceding one, we may find the verb in the final position.

---

51 Kuhn, "Zur Wortstellung":50.
52 Kuhn, "Zur Wortstellung":63.
53 Kuhn, "Zur Wortstellung":50.
54 Cf. Delbrück, *Syntax II*, fn 14. By contrast, in Modern German the particle itself determines the position of the verb, so that, for example, *denn* and *weil*, 'because', require different word-orders.

Her cuom micel sciphere on West Walas, 7 hie to anum gecierdon, 7 wiþ Ecgbryht West Seaxna cyning winnende wæron; þa he þæt hierde, 7 mid fierde ferde, 7 him wiþ feaht æt Hengest tune. (*Chronicle* 855 A.D.)

'In this year many fleets came to Cornwall, and they joined forces with the Cornishmen and prepared to wage war against Egbert, King of Wessex. Then the news reached him, and he marched with an army, and met them in battle at Hingston'

Presumably the order *þa hierde he þæt* would have been equally acceptable, but would have had the effect of separating the following clauses from the preceding ones; this the author did not wish to do, for it would divide the narrative into two parts.

Kuhn associates the contrast in verb-position between bound and independent clauses with Wackernagel's Law. According to this 'Law', the unaccented verb of the main (i.e., independent) clause is placed in the enclitic position, near the beginning of the clause but after the first accented word, and the verb of the subordinate (i.e., bound) clause remained in the final position. Kuhn investigated the Germanic alliterative verse and found that the verb of the bound clause was rarely in anacrusis (*Senkung*) but that of the dependent clause was frequently there; "it therefore seems certain to me that the finite verb in the Germanic bound clause once had a considerably stronger accent than in the independent clause."[55]

For Kuhn, then, the independent clause verb is a reflex of an earlier unstressed enclitic verb. My term EXTRA-SEQUENTIAL, however, refers to the reflex of an emphatic, originally clause-initial verb. The verb in anacrusis is usually a light verb reflecting an original unmarked verb, but may also be a light verb which, although marked, has been attracted by its weight into the category of unstressed elements. According to Kuhn's hypothesis the independent verb should never be stressed sufficiently to alliterate; and yet it is precisely when the verb is initial that it most frequently shares alliteration, whereas the assumed 'unaccented' verb in the bound clause never alliterates. Lehmann assumes:

a hierarchy of stress, such that the strongest fell on the key alliteration (i.e. the first alliterating syllable in the second half-line), the next strongest on the first alliteration of the first half-line; the second stress of the first half-line was only slightly less stressed than this, but the last stress of the line was considerably weaker than the others.[56]

The finite verb of Kuhn's bound clause occurs most often in the last — and weakest — stress in the line. By contrast, the verb of the independent clause occurs typically in the first stress of the first half-line, often alliterates, and occasionally bears the main alliteration of its half-line, as in the following examples:

> Gemunde þa se goda, mæg Higelaces (*Beowulf* 758)
> 'Then the good man, the kinsman of Higelac, remembered'
> (lif langerun huil.) Lagun tha uuardos (*Heliand* 5802)
> '(The guardians (of the tomb) lay'

---

[55]   Kuhn, "Zur Wortstellung":56.
[56]   Winfred P. Lehmann, *The Alliteration of Old Saxon Poetry* (Oslo, Aschehoug, 1953), p. 32.

Apparently, then, if we except the inherently light verbs, the accentuation of the verb in independent and bound clauses is the opposite of what would be expected from Wackernagel's Law. If, however, we assume that the verb of the Germanic independent clause reflects, not the unaccented main-clause verb as seen in Sanskrit, but the marked, accented verb in head position, the position and stronger stress of these verbs is more readily explained.

Wackernagel's Law is not without application to the position of the verb in the clause in Germanic. The distinction between a main clause and a subordinate clause in Proto-Germanic was that in the neutral clause the verb of a main clause was free to be placed in enclisis to the first stressed sentence constituent, whereas the verb of a subordinate clause did not have this possibility. The neutral position of the verb in all sequential clauses was the final one,[57] but in main clauses a light verb could appear in second position even in a narrative sequence, provided it was not in a subordinate clause,[58] as in the following passage:

þa feng Ælfred Æþelwulfing his broþur to Wesseaxna rice; 7 þæs ymb anna monaþ gefeaht Ælfred cyning wiþ alne þone here æt Wiltune, 7 hine longe on dæg gefliemde, 7 þa Deniscan ahton wæl stowe geweald; 7 þæs geares wurdon .viiii. folc gefeaht gefohten wiþ þone here on þa cynerice be suþan Temese, 7 butan þam þe him Ælfred þæs cyninges broþur, 7 anlipig aldormon, 7 cyninges þegnas oft rade onridon þe mon na ne rimde, 7 þæs geares wærun ofslægene .viiii. eorlas 7 an cyning. (*Chronicle* 871 A.D.)

'Then his brother Alfred, son of Aethelwulf, succeeded to the kingdom of Wessex. And one month later King Alfred fought at Wilton with a small force against the entire Danish army, and for a long time during the day held them off, but the Danes won the day. In the course of the year nine general battles were fought against the Danes in Surrey, not to mention the frequent forays which Alfred (,) the king's brother, a single alderman, and the king's thanes rode out on, and which no one ever counted; and during the year nine earls and one king were slain'.

Although the positions of the verbs in main and subordinate clauses in the earliest Germanic dialects contrast to the limited extent that the main clause verb may appear in the enclitic position, it is not clear whether the greater freedom of the main clause verb was traditional or whether the subordinate clause verb remained in historical times more strongly stressed than the main clause verb. The alliterative verse is inconclusive; there is no discernable difference in stress between the final verb of a main clause and a subordinate clause. We find no instances of voicing of voiceless fricatives which might reflect the operation of Verner's Law in the consonantism of an unaccented main-clause verb. My investigation of the written accents in Otfrid's *Evangelienbuch* does not support Bonfante's contention of an accentual contrast between main and subordinate clause verbs in Old High German.[59] The most reasonable conclusion

---

[57] If the extra-sequential clause is considered to be 'marked', and the sequential clause 'unmarked', this contrast in basic word orders can be regarded as the consequence of a cross-conjunction elimination of the marking feature. Such an analysis would seem to be especially appropriate as an explanation of the 'sequential imperative' phenomenon discussed above, pp. 48-49. Conjunction reduction rules in Indo-European are discussed in Kiparsky, "Tense and Mood".

[58] The appearance of subordinate clause verbs in second position, usually when light, is a later, analogical one, which in English is characteristic of the later language.

[59] Bonfante, "Proposizione": 9. It is admittedly possible to find instances of accented subordinate

would be that the difference in verb position between the main and subordinate clauses in the Germanic dialects reflects the operation of Wackernagel's Law in Proto-Indo-European, but that the greater mobility of the main clause verb does not necessarily signify the continuation of an accentual contrast in Proto-Germanic.

b. *The Enclitic Verb*

In the first part of this section I discussed the Proto-Germanic clause-final verb, and suggested that in main clauses it was in complementary distribution with the reflex of the Proto-Indo-European enclitic verb. I will now discuss in more detail the syntax of the light verb in Proto-Germanic.

The enclitic verb in Proto-Indo-European was of light weight, that is, it consisted of only one or two syllables, and of low lexical yield, that is, the clause in which it stood was intelligible without it. The verb *to be*, for example, is typically enclitic in many of the older Indo-European dialects, as are verbs of making, writing and dedicating in inscriptions, and verbs of saying in colloquy. The omission of the verb altogether may have been an alternative to placing it in enclisis; the verb *to be* is often omitted in copular equations.[60]

Delbrück asociated the increased frequency of the enclitic verb in the earlier Germanic dialects with the rise of auxiliation.[61] In many Indo-European dialects differences of tense and aspect came to be expressed by auxiliary verbs rather than by inflection of the verb stem. These auxiliary verbs were light and possessed little or no lexical content, but served as bearers of verbal inflection; since tense, aspect and mood were frequently predictable in a sentence, the auxiliary verbs often appeared in sentence-second position, or were omitted. The third person verb, which was the unmarked member of the verbal paradigm, was especially often omitted.[62]

In the Germanic dialects omission of the verb was rare. On the contrary, we find in the Gothic Bible many examples of the verb *to be* inserted where the Greek original omits it, for example *þata auk ist wilja gudis* τοῦτο γὰρ θέλημα θεοῦ 'for that is the will of God' (*Thessalonians* II, 5, 18). In main clauses, the light verbs and verbs of low lexical content are often found in the second position. In early Old English prose the auxiliaries *wesan*, *weorþan* and *habban* regularly are placed in this position:

---

clause verbs in Otfrid. But, although, like Bonfante, I have not carried out a statistical count, there seem to me to be no fewer examples of accented main clause verbs, and many examples of unaccented verbs in both types of clause. It naturally follows that there will be a NON-SIGNIFICANT number of instances in which the main clause verb is unaccented and the subordinate verb is accented, as in that quoted by Bonfante (Otfrid, II, 14, 95).

[60] Cf. Ernst Kieckers, *Die Stellung des Verbums in Griechischen und in den verwandten Sprachen* (Strassburg, Trübner, 1911), p. 80.
[61] Delbrück, *Germanische Syntax II*, p. 15.
[62] Cf. Hirt, *Grammatik*, vol. VII, p. 20.

he wæs on Breten londe geboren (*Chronicle* 381 A.D.)
'he was born in Britain'

Her Bregowine wæs to erce bisc: gehadod to Ste: Michaeles tide (*Chronicle* 759 A.D.)
'In this year Bregwin was consecrated Archbishop at Michaelmastide'

Her Mul wearþ on Cent forbærned (*Chronicle* 678 A.D.)
'In this year Mul was burned to death in Kent'

7 þær wearþ Sidroc earl ofslægen (*Chronicle* 871 A.D.)
'and there Earl Sidroc was slain'

Ac hie hæfdon þa heora stemn ge setence, 7 hiora mete ge notudne (*Chronicle* 894 A.D.)
'But their term of military duty had expired, and they had eaten up all their food'

Although the pattern is not invariable, we frequently find that when the auxiliary verb is in the enclitic position, the dependent non-finite part of the verb is at or near the end of the clause, as in the above examples. In other words, the part of the verb which bears the semantic content of the clause in main clauses is clause-final.

In alliterative verse, auxiliary verbs are often found not only in the second position, but also in the clause-initial position, where they are in anacrusis to the alliterating syllables. Such clause-initial light verbs shared the position of the emphatic verb as already described in section B. 1.; they are distinguishable from the emphatic verb by their inherent lightness. The shift of the unstressed verb towards the beginning of the clause may have contributed to the disappearance of the initial position of the verb as an emphatic alternative to the final verb. In the later Germanic dialects the absolute initial position of the verb is preserved only in specialized functions such as the imperative construction.[63] Often in alliterative verse, and sometimes in prose, it is impossible to distinguish positionally between a light verb in anacrusis and a clause-initial emphatic verb. In both prose and verse, the light verb may appear in clause-initial position:

hæfde se cyning his fierd on tu to numen (*Chronicle* 894 A.D.)
'the king had divided his army into two'

wæs Hesten þa þær cumen mid his herge (*Chronicle* 894 A.D.)
'Hesten had arrived there with his forces'

(ellenmærþum). Hæfde East-Denum
Geatmecga leod gilp gelæsted (*Beowulf* 828-29)
'The chief of the Goths had made a boast to the East-Danes'

(fuse to farenne;) wolde feor þanon
cuma collenferhð ceoles neosan (*Beowulf* 1805-06)
'Far from there the bold-spirited guest wanted to go to seek out the ship'

sceal hringnaca ofer heafu bringan
lac ond luftacen (*Beowulf* 1862-63)
'over the seas, the ringed ship shall bring gifts and tributes'

---

[63] The falling together of the proclitic and the emphatic verb at the head of the clause might have led to a generalization of the initial position. This did not in fact happen in any Germanic dialect. In Old Norse, however, the clause-initial verb is so common that it has been assumed to be the normal one, cf. the discussion in Heusler, *Elementarbuch*, p. 173. Heusler assumes that the initial verbs in Old Norse mostly represent the spread of the emphatic type, and does not mention the possibility that many of them may be light verbs in proclisis.

From these and other examples it may be assumed that Proto-Germanic inherited enclisis of the light verb from Proto-Indo-European, just as it inherited enclisis of certain particles, and that, like the particles, the light verb could appear under unspecified circumstances in proclisis to the first autonomous sentence-element.

Just as certain particles were invariably enclitic, and never appeared in proclisis, so there were certain verbs which were always placed after the first important word of the clause. In *Beowulf*, the form *maþelode* 'quoth, inquit, aiit' is found only in enclisis, and never alliterates, e.g.:

> Hroðgar maþelode, helm Scyldinga (*Beowulf* 371)
> 'Hrothgar, lord of the Scyldings, said:...'
> Wulfgar maþelode — þæt wæs Wendla leod (*Beowulf* 348)
> 'Wulfgar said (who was lord of the Wendels):'

The lines in which *maþelode* occurs tend to be stylized. The first one cited above occurs three times (*Beowulf* 371, 456, 1321), and the line *Beowulf maþelode, bearn Ecgþeowes* no less than seven times (*Beowulf* 529, 631, 957, 1383, 1473, 1651, 1817). We may therefore assume that the form retained in archaic formulas its Proto-Germanic positional characteristics, and that the use of the word in poetry was always modelled on these formulas. In a similar way the archaizing Modern English word *quoth* traditionally has an inverted enclitic subject *quoth-he, quotha* (cf. Old Saxon *quathie*). The form *maþelode* is, it is true, not light, but it fulfills the condition of having a low semantic yield, for its only function is to introduce direct speech (*maþelode* is never followed by a dependent clause of indirect speech).

C. SUMMARY OF SECTION II

Proto-Germanic inherited the Proto-Indo-European contrast in verb position between a neutral and a marked clause. In both periods the basic syntagm was: final verb in the neutral, initial verb in the marked clause. At a very early time, however, probably already during the Proto-Indo-European period, certain light and semantically redundant verbs could appear in enclisis to the first autonomous element in the sentence. The enclitic position became in Proto-Germanic an important alternative to the final position, especially when the growing number of periphrastic constructions increased the frequency of light auxiliary verbs.

When the finite verb increasingly tended to appear in the second position in neutral clauses, the former maximal positional differentiation between the marked and the unmarked or neutral verb was reduced: the two types of verb were no longer at opposite ends of the clause. When, later, the enclitic verb could be placed at the head of the clause in proclisis to the first autonomous element, all positional contrast between the marked and the neutral verb was removed. In the later history of the Germanic dialects the initial verb is associated with specialized functions: imperative, interrogative and conditional constructions.

The conditions under which the initial verb was used in Proto-Germanic accord closely with those which other comparative evidence permits us to reconstruct for Proto-Indo-European. Yet the specialization of word-order for a limited number of constructions is a development of the separate Indo-European dialects. The imperative, for example, is by no means universally characterized by the initial verb, but frequently has the initial verb because of its emphasis on the verbal idea. The specialization of the initial verb as a mark of the imperative belongs to the Proto-Germanic period. Similarly, the yes-no questions were not originally marked by the initial verb, but by intonation; the only syntactic mark of interrogation was that a specific word to be interrogated was placed at the head of the clause, with or without an emphatic particle. If, as frequently happened, the whole clause was to be interrogated, the finite verb itself was placed at the head of the clause. In Gothic this situation may have still prevailed; but there is enough evidence from the other Germanic dialects for us to assume that the clause-initial verb was in Proto-Germanic already an important sign of interrogation.

The interrogative and imperative constructions have in common, apart from the verb position, the property of being external to a sequence of sentences in a narrative. The clause-initial verb is characteristic of all such extra-sequential clauses, including successive clauses in vivid narative, where each incident is presented as a unity. In the oldest alliterative verse, for example *Beowulf* and the *Heliand*, new episodes and other changes of topic often have the initial verb, and this verb frequently carries part of the alliteration. In the oldest Germanic prose, the *þa* + Verb construction performs an identical function.

With intra-sequential clauses we must distinguish between main and subordinate clauses. In Proto-Indo-European an accentual contrast had existed between the verb in a main clause and that in a subordinate clause. The lighter accentuation of the main clause verb permitted it to be attracted into the enclitic position, whereas the heavier accentuation of the subordinate clause verb did not permit this shift. The exact accentual conditions are not clear, nor can we be certain that the accentual contrast itself was inherited into Proto-Germanic. The positional contrast between a main and a subordinate clause verb is, however, certain: only the main clause verb may appear in enclisis in the oldest Germanic dialects.

IV

THE SYNTAX OF ADVERBIAL AND SUBSTANTIVAL GROUPS

The sentence elements whose syntax is discussed in this chapter are essentially the class of so-called 'heavy' elements, those which characteristically bear the principal stress in alliterative verse, and whose position in the clause was most mobile. The categories involved here are nouns, adverbs and adjectives. For convenience, a subclass of adverbs which are not normally 'heavy', the pronominal adverbs, is also included here.

Statements about the surface syntax of proto-languages are necessarily more tentative than those about phonology and morphology, but there are especially severe difficulties in dealing with elements which were subject to perhaps rather subtle positional changes in accordance with factors of focus and 'emphasis', as was the case with the elements treated here. Stylistic considerations probably played an important role, making the identification of basic positions for these constituents particularly hazardous. In the following discussion, most of the examples are taken from Old English. Gothic affords practically no evidence which is independent of the *Vorlage*, and here as elsewhere it would be hard to exaggerate the caution with which the Wulfilan texts should be used to make inferences about Proto-Germanic sentence structure. Old Norse, in generalizing the second and front position of the verb, has also progressed further in the direction of freedom of word order. Yet Old English itself, although generally more conservative than the other dialects, also displays considerable flexibility in the arrangement of adverbial and nominal elements, and the flexibility should also be assumed for Proto-Germanic. A few tendencies may be pointed out. I will begin by discussing the internal structure of the noun phrase, and then take up ordering within the sentence of adverbial and functional constituents (subject, object, indirect object).

A. THE STRUCTURE OF THE NOUN PHRASE

1. *Adjective and Noun*

Both the prior and the post position of the adjective are found in the early Germanic dialects, but the neutral position appears to have been the one preceding the noun.

In Old English, for example, the post position is found only with proper names:

> Guþlac se halga (*Chronicle* 714 A.D.)
> 'St. Guthlac'

and even here the pattern is not invariable, e.g.:

> se eadga Petrus (*Chronicle* 35 A.D.)
> 'the blessed Peter'

In Old Norse, more variety was possible, and the distinction between the two positions was distinctive. The preceding adjective was descriptive, whereas the following adjective was restrictive.[1] This distinction is not easily correlated with the distinction between strong and weak adjective declensions, because the distribution of the two sets of endings in the earliest Germanic dialects is already to a large extent dependent on the presence or absence of a definite article or demonstrative, and no clear consistency is found in the use of strong or weak endings in the small number of exceptions to this dependency. In Old Norse, both strong and weak adjectives could appear before or after the noun. The generally greater flexibility of word order in Old Norse, taken together with the regular preceding position of the adjective in the other dialects, would point to the prior position as the original one in Proto-Germanic, but the possibility that both positions were available in Proto-Indo-European should not be overlooked; Brugmann observes:

The prior position of the adjective seems at all times to have been in general more frequent when the adjective, because of its semantic content, expresses a quality which is inherent and characteristic, without any thought of other entities which do not have this quality. Whilst the adjective in this position completes the concept of the noun, the posterior position serves to make distinctions.[2]

If this distinction holds good for both Proto-Indo-European and Proto-Germanic, an original syntactic connection may have existed between a restrictive adjective with weak endings following the noun, and a descriptive adjective with strong endings preceding the noun. The syntactic change accomplished in Old Norse would then have been one in which weak endings became associated with the newly formed definite articles, and the positional distinction was retained.

2. *Adnominal Genitive and Noun*

In Germanic, a distinction must be made between the possessive and the partitive use of the genitive,[3] in order to account for the positional contrast between phrases such as

---

[1] "The postponed adjective forms a colon for itself, the preceding adjective draws the noun to it in one accent group. In the postponed adjective there is more of a predicative function (expressible at times by a relative clause), in the preceding adjective the concept is more unitary (similar to a compound)" Heusler, *Elementarbuch*, p. 177.

[2] Karl Brugmann, *Die Syntax des einfachen Satzes im Indogermanischen* (Berlin, de Gruyter, 1925) pp. 109-10.

[3] Behaghel, *Deutsche Syntax*, vol. 4, 177-94.

> on þæs wifes gebærum (*Chronicle* 755 A.D.)
> 'at the woman's cries'

and:

> þone mæstan dæl þæs ealandes (*Chronicle* 47 A.D.)
> 'the greater part of the island'

In Old English prose, the possessive genitive regularly precedes the noun, and very few exceptions are found to this rule. In Old Saxon also, the preceding genitive is consistent, except that it normally follows when the possessing noun is 'God' or 'Christ':

> iro druhtines uuord (*Heliand* 2857)
> 'their Lord's words'

but:

> the iungaron Cristes (*Heliand* 3151)
> 'Christ's disciples'
> helag stemne godes (*Heliand* 3147)
> 'the holy voice of God'

In Old High German poetry, and in prose where no immediate influence of Latin has to be assumed, genitives also precede the noun:[4]

> dhazs almahtiga gotes chiruni dhera gotliihhun Christes chiburdi (Isidor, *Contra Iudeos*)
> 'the almighty mystery of God of Christ's divine birth'
> Siones dohter (Isidor, *Contra Indeos*)
> 'Daughter of Zion'

(where, in the last example, the Latin model has *filia Sion*);

> Hiltibrantes sunu (*Hildebrandslied* 1.14)
> 'Hildebrand's son'

In West Germanic, in other words, the possessive genitive has a consistent position before the possessed noun.

In Gothic, the picture is contradictory. Koppitz's data[5] show an almost exactly equal division between the prior and post-nominal position of the possessive genitive in examples where either no precedent or the opposite precedent exists in the *Vorlage*. Compound nouns with an inflected first member (the so-called *unechte Komposita*) such as *baurgswaddjus* 'city wall', however, may give evidence of an original neutral ordering, and the variety of positions may be a later development of Gothic and the Nordic languages.

For Old Norse, Heusler states: "The genitive determining the noun customarily follows it (*pflegt nachzustehen*)",[6] yet there are so many exceptions to the 'rule' that free ordering is more likely. In patronymics, which are likely to represent an archaic type of ordering, the (genitive) name always precedes the word for 'son': *Gunnarsson*,

---

[4] See p. 23 for the primary source for *Contra Iudeos*.
[5] A. Koppitz, "Gotische Wortstellung", *ZfdPh* 32 (1900):435-38.
[6] Heusler, *Elementarbuch*, p. 177.

Skjodolfsdottur, etc. Similarly, geographical names, e.g., *Hrafnkelsdalr* and many other examples. Both of these types parallel the inflected type of noun compound. In Old Swedish the order genitive-noun is almost invariable in the oldest documents (the West Gutnic laws), e.g., *mæþ Guz miskun* 'with God's grace', *bondæ sun* 'a yeoman's son'.[7] The early Runic monuments whose interpretation is fairly secure show the following instances of genitives preceding the noun:

> magoR minas staina (*Vetteland Stone*)[8]
> 'my son's stone'
>
> Hnabudas hlaiwa (*Bø Stone*)[9]
> 'Hnabud's grave-mound'
>
> ...an waruR (*Tomstad Stone*)[10]
> '...'s tomb'
>
> Hariþulfs stainaR (*Rävsal Stone*)[11]
> 'Hariþulf's stone'

Against these examples there is one with a clear following genitive:

> þewar Godagas (*Valsfjord Rock Inscription*)[12]
> 'follower of Godag'

The predominant pattern in the language of the Runic inscriptions appears to be GENITIVE — NOUN, but the evidence is not complete. The impression is that an original order genitive-noun was shifting to a free order in the North Germanic territory of Runic, Gothic and Nordic, with the original pattern being preserved in compounds.

3. *Apposition and Noun*

The order of a proper name and a noun in apposition to it is quite consistent in the early Germanic dialects. In the Old English *Chronicle*, in which titles such as king, alderman, abbot, bishop, pope, etc., abound, there are numerous illustrative examples, e.g.:

> Petrus se apostel (*Chronicle* 35 A.D.)
> 'the apostle Peter'
>
> Titus Uespassianus sunu (*Chronicle* 71 A.D.)
> 'Titus, son of Vespasian'
>
> in Paþma þam ealond (*Chronicle* 84 A.D.)
> 'on the Isle of Pathmos'
>
> Gregorius papa (*Chronicle* 597 A.D.)
> 'Pope Gregory'

---

[7] Elias Wessen, ed., *Fornsvenka Texter. Mit Förklaringar och Ordlista* (Andra, utökade Upplagen, Stockholm, Svenska Bokförlaget, 1959), pp. 6-7.
[8] Krause and Jankuhn, *Die Runeninschriften*, 136-39.
[9] Krause and Jankuhn, *Die Runeninschriften*, p. 181.
[10] Krause and Jankuhn, *Die Runeninschriften*, pp. 182-83.
[11] Krause and Jankuhn, *Die Runeninschriften*, pp. 183-85.
[12] Krause and Jankuhn, *Die Runeninschriften*, pp. 123-25.
[13] Heusler, *Elementarbuch*, p. 182.

> Edwine Norðhymbra cyning (*Chronicle* 597 A.D.)
> 'Edwin, King of the Northumbrians'

Similar patterns are described for Old Norse by Heusler,[13] with examples such as: *Olafr konungr* 'King Olaf'; *Gizorr biskop* 'Bishop Gizorr'. From Old High German we may adduce:

> Hiltibrant, Heribrantes suno (*Hildebrandslied* 44)
> 'Hildebrand, son of Heribrand'

And from Old Saxon:

> an Galileo land (*Heliand* 5955)
> 'to the land of Galilee'
>
> mahtig Krist,
> the godo godes sunu (*Heliand* 2846-47)
> 'mighty Christ, the good son of God'

It might be pointed out here, in anticipation of remarks on the typological ordering of elements in the noun phrase, that geographical names involving a proper noun and a topographical feature have the same positional characteristics as appositional phrases, as in several of the above examples. The ordering 'Name-Topographical feature' is confirmed by compounds such as *Sceap-ige* (Old English) 'Shep Island, Sheppey'.

4. *Pronominal Modifiers*

In Old English, and in Old High German, the demonstrative or article consistently precedes the noun, as does the possessive pronoun. In Old Saxon, the possessive precedes the noun with a few exceptions, most of them vocatives such as *gesiðos mine* 'my companions' (*Heliand* 1361); if the possessive is the genitive of the pronoun, it invariably precedes, e.g., *is lif* 'his life' (*Heliand* 4104). If the possessed noun is modified by an adjective following it, the possessive pronoun follows the noun and not the adjective; thus the formula *fro min the godo* (*passim*), which contrasts with the order preceding the noun. Both patterns are exemplified in the following:

> 'ni thunkid mi this somi thing,' quað he,
> 'fro min the godo, that thu mine foti thuahes
> mid them thinun helagan handun' (*Heliand* 4508-10)
> 'I consider it unseemly,' he said, 'my good master, for you to wash my feet with your holy hands'

In North Germanic and the Runic monuments this pattern has developed further. Possessives appear behind the noun, as in the *Kjøvelik Stone* inscription:

> ek Hagusta(l)daR hlaaiwido magu minino[14]
> 'I, Hagustald, curied my son'

and generally in Old Norse. In Old Swedish, both positions are possible:

---

14   Krause and Jankuhn, *Die Runeninschriften*, p. 179.

utæn sins biskups orloff[15]
'without his bishop's consent'

fore konungi sinum[16]
'before his king'

But the possessive intervenes between noun and postponed adjective; thus Heusler describes for Old Norse the orders NOUN — POSSESSIVE — ADJECTIVE:

af gǫfgom frændom minom
'of my distinguished relatives'

and Noun-Possessive-Adjective:

spiót hans et gøþa
'his good spear'

but no ordering NOUN — ADJECTIVE — POSSESSIVE.[17] The *Opedal Stone* inscription suggests a similar ordering in Runic:

swestar minu liubu
'my dear sister'[18]

Koppitz's data[19] suggest that in Gothic, too, the possessive regularly followed the noun; this is the order even against the precedent of the Vorlage, e.g. *haubiþ þein*, σου ἡ κεφαλή 'thy head' (*Matthew* 6, 17).

The demonstrative preceded the noun in Gothic, and in the West Germanic languages. Koppitz shows the article and demonstrative *sa, þata, so* almost invariably preceding the noun, while *jains* follows the noun only when the *Vorlage* also has the order NOUN — DEMONSTRATIVE.[20] In North Germanic, although the demonstrative generally precedes the noun, suffixed articles have been developed, e.g., *maðrenn*. This pattern is usually assumed to have arisen from phrases such as *maðr enn gamle* 'the old man', and such an origin is supported by the fact that the article is not suffixed if the noun is preceded by an adjective. Hence the possible orders of demonstrative, noun and adjective were *D-A-N*, or *N-D-A*, but not *N-A-D*. In Gothic we find one instance in which these three elements are combined with no precedent from the Greek *Vorlage*:

jah afsloh imma auso þata taihswo,
καὶ ἀφεῖλεν αὐτοῦ τὸ ὠτίον
'and struck off his right ear'
(*Mark* 17, 47)

The absence in the early Germanic dialects of a pattern NOUN — ADJECTIVE — DEMONSTRATIVE/POSSESSIVE indicates that both demonstratives and possessives originally preceded their noun, and is incidental evidence also of the neutral position of the

---

[15]   Wessén, *Fornsvenska Texter*, pp. 11.
[16]   Wessén, *Fornsvenska Texter*, pp. 13-14.
[17]   Heusler, *Elementarbuch*, p. 179.
[18]   Krause and Jankuhn, *Die Runeninschriften*, p. 75.
[19]   Koppitz, "Gotische Wortstellung":444-45.
[20]   Koppitz, "Gotische Wortstellung":446-49.

preceding adjective. From a typological point of view we expect to find demonstratives at the periphery of the surface noun phrase and the adjective intervening between demonstrative and head noun, i.e., either *D-A-N* or *N-A-D*.[21] It is more intuitive to suppose that the demonstrative and adjective were postponed appositionally as a group than that the original order ADJECTIVE — DEMONSTRATIVE was reversed against the prevailing template of 'natural' word order.

5. *Hyperbaton*

The syntactic pattern of hyperbaton is exemplified in phrases of the following kind:

> þæs oþres eorles broþor Ohteres (*Chronicle* 918 A.D.)
> 'the brother of Ohter, the other earl'
>
> Ælfredes sweoster cyninges (*Chronicle* 888 A.D.)
> 'King Alfred's sister'
>
> 7 feng Æþelbryht to allum þam rice his broþur (*Chronicle* 860 A.D.)
> 'and his brother Æþelbryht succeeded to the whole kingdom'
>
> se æþela papa 7 se halga (*Chronicle* 814 A.D.)
> 'the noble and holy pope'

One part of a complex noun phrase is shifted to another position in the sentence, forming a discontinuous constituent. The rule of hyperbaton is very ancient. Hirt, after describing examples in Indo-European, remarks: "There is such striking agreement on this point between Greek, Latin and Indic that one can scarcely doubt the prehistoric age of hyperbaton."[22]

The agreement between the three traditional branches of Germanic shows the rule to go back to Proto-Germanic. The construction is described for Old Norse by Heusler,[23] with examples such as:

> Ragnars sonr loþbrókar
> 'the son of Ragnar Shaggy-breeks'
>
> fritt liþ ok miket
> 'fair and strong crew'

One example is even found in Gothic, against the *Vorlage*:

> unselja skalk jah lata,
> πονηρὲ δοῦλε, (*Luke* 19, 22)
> 'wicked and lazy servant'

The Old English construction involving two conjoined subjects is probably also connected with the phenomenon of hyperbaton:

Her Cynewulf benam Sigebryht his rices 7 West Seaxna wiotan for unrytum dædum (*Chronicle* 755 A.D.)
'In this year, Cynewulf and the West Saxon elders deprived Sigebryht of his kingdom for wrong-doing'

---

[21] Cf. Greenberg, ed., *Universals*, p. 87.
[22] Hirt, *Grammatik*, vol. VII, pp. 231-32.
[23] Heusler, *Elementarbuch*, 177-79. Cf. also Neckel, *Edda*, p. 14.

Two competing explanations seem possible for the phenomenon. The break-down of an earlier rigid word-order may have had as one of its consequences a preference for less complex phrases, especially where several modifying constituents were placed before their head constituent. A second argument could be constructed along the lines of the "gapping" rule,[24] and hyperbaton could be regarded as the absence of a rule which would move a modifier whose head had been deleted by 'gapping'. The first of these explanations would accord rather neatly with the hypothesis that Proto-Germanic was a SOV language in transition, with modifiers which increasingly tended to detach themselves from their regular position before their head. It should be observed that all major categories are involved in hyperbaton, including adverbs:

> ...7 lytle hwile heold 7 ungefealice (*Chronicle* 755 A.D.)
> 'and (he) held (the throne) for a short while and unhappily'

and predicate adjectives:

> swa hwelc swa þonne gearo wearþ 7 radost (*Chronicle* 755 A.D.)
> 'whichever of them were ready and swiftest'

The question whether this explanation can also be used to account for 'embedded' structures such as genitives and attributive adjectives must be left open.

B. THE POSITIONAL SYNTAX OF NOUN PHRASES

For the reasons stated earlier, most of the examples illustrating the positional syntax of nominal groups will be taken from Old English. I shall be concerned in this section with the functional constituents SUBJECT, OBJECT, INDIRECT OBJECT, COMPLEMENT, and also with some types of adverbials.

1. *The Noun Phrase as Subject*

The position of the noun phrase as subject can be described in relation to the verb and the light elements. In all clauses, the neutral position of the subject noun phrase in relation to the noun objects (direct and indirect) is prior to the object. Such an ordering is, of course, to be expected, since it is, according to Greenberg,[25] a near-universal. In verb-final clauses the nominal subject is placed as a rule after the light elements and before heavy adverbs and the verb:

> 7 hiene þa Cynewulf on Andred adræfde (*Chronicle* 755 A.D.)
> 'and then Cynewulf exiled him to Andred'
>
> oþ þæt hiene an swan ofstang æt Pryfetes flod (*Chronicle* 755 A.D.)
> 'until a herdsman stabbed him at Priffet's Flood'
>
> 7 þa se gerefa þærto rad (*Chronicle* 787 A.D.)
> 'and when the reeve went there'

[24] Ross, "Gapping".
[25] Greenberg, *Universals*, p. 76.

> 7 hæþne men ærest on Sceap ige ofer winter sæton (*Chronicle* 855 A.D.)
> 'and the heathen men for the first time spent the winter on Sheppey'

In clauses with initial verb, including those introduced by *þa*, the nominal subject usually follows both the verb and any light elements in the clause:

> Hæfde hine Penda adrifenne (*Chronicle* 658 A.D.)
> 'Penda had expelled him'
>
> þa ge wraðede hine se ar.b. Landfranc (*Chronicle* 1070 A.D.)
> 'then Archbishop Landfranc became angry'
>
> þa gegaderade Ælfred cyning his fierd (*Chronicle* 894 A.D.)
> 'King Alfred gathered his forces'
>
> ne com se here oftor eall ute of þæm setum þonne tuwwa (*Chronicle* 894 A.D.)
> 'the army finally made only two sorties from the camp'
>
> ne wearþ þær forþon an Bret to lafe (*Chronicle* 494 A.D.)
> 'for only one Celt remained alive'

The syntax of the nominal phrase subject in verb-second clauses is the same as in verb-initial clauses, except that the subject can precede the verb:

> 7 Burgræd Miercna cyning 7 his wiotan bædon Æþered
> West Seaxna cyning 7 Ælfred his broþur þæt hie
> him gefultumadon... (*Chronicle* 868 A.D.)
> 'and Burgred, king of the Mercians, and his councillors requested Ethelred and his brother Alfred to help them...'
>
> 7 þy ilcan geare East Engla cyning 7 seo þeod gesohte
> Ecgbryht cyning him to friþ (*Chronicle* 823 A.D.)
> 'and the same year the king of the East Anglians and the people sought to make peace with King Egbert'

2. *The Nominal Phrase as Complement of the Verb*

a. *Direct Object and Indirect Object*

i. *Relative Order of Direct and Indirect Object*

If a direct and an indirect object occur together in the same clause, the direct object normally follows the indirect object, e.g.:

> 7 hie saldon hiera tuæm neffum Stufe 7 Wihtgare Wiehte
> ealond (*Chronicle* 537 A.D.)
> 'and they gave the Isle of Wight to their two nephews Stufe and Wihtgar'
>
> 7 East Engle hæfdon Ælfrede cyninge aþas geseald (*Chronicle* 894 A.D.)
> 'and the East Angles had given King Alfred oaths'
>
> Do thinun iungorun so self (*Heliand* 1594b)
> 'do the same for your disciples'

ii. *Position of Direct and Indirect Object*

In verb-final clauses the objects of the verb followed the subject, and had the same position relative to other elements as the subject, i.e., they were placed after the light elements and before the heavy adverbs and the verb:

7 hiera se æþeling gehwelcum feoh 7 feorh gebæd (*Chronicle* 755 A.D.)
'and the prince offered to each one of them life and property'

huo thiu engilo craft alomahtigna god
swiðo werðlico uuordun lobodun (*Heliand* 416-17)
'how the host of angels most reverently praised almighty God'

In verb-second clauses considerable stylistic variation is found in all the dialects. I will not give examples of all the possible permutations, such as SUBJECT — VERB — OBJECT, ADVERB — VERB — SUBJECT..., etc. As many scholars have pointed out, in the recorded dialects the final verb is less frequent when both subject and object are Nouns,[26] and in the later Germanic dialects the order Subject-Verb-Object became the rule for both nominal and pronominal elements in a main clause. In the oldest dialects a frequent pattern is NOMINAL SUBJECT — VERB — NOMINAL OBJECT:

Thia modar uuiopun
kindiungaro qualm (*Heliand* 744-45)
'The mothers bewailed the death of their children'

ek hagusta(l)daR hl(a)aiwido magu minino
'I, a warrior, buried my boy' (*Kjølevik Stone*)[27]

Her Ceolnoþ ærce bisc: onfeng pallium (*Chronicle* 831 A.D.)
'In this year Archbishop Ceolnoth received the pallium'

Her Cyneheard ofslog Cynewulf cyning (*Chronicle* 784 A.D.)
'In this year Cynehard slew King Cynewulf'

In verb-initial sentences the subject normally follows the verb directly, but light elements may be inserted between the verb and the nominal subject, e.g.:

hæfde hine Penda adrifenne (*Chronicle* 658 A.D.)
'Penda had expelled him'
Habda im uualdand god
....
fasto bifolhan (*Heliand* 20-22)
'Almighty God had...firmly exhorted them'

b. *As Complement of Substantive Verb*

In this section I will treat the complement not only of the verb *to be*, but also of other verbs followed by a noun phrase in the nominative; I therefore include verbs of *naming*, but will exclude from discussion the syntagms of the form *þam was nama Natanþeod* 'his name was Natantheod' (*Chronicle* 508 A.D.).

As I have indicated,[28] the verbs *to be* and *to become* in the oldest Germanic dialects were already found chiefly in the second (enclitic) position in the sentence. The nominal complement of *to be* and *to become* does not differ syntactically from the object noun

---

[26] Cf. Schneider, *Die Stellungstypen*, p. 41; Behaghel, *Deutsche Syntax*, vol. IV, p. 14; Fourquet, *L'ordre*, p. 290.
[27] Krause and Jankuhn, *Die Runeninschriften*, p. 173.
[28] Cf. p. 56; *to be* and *to become* were light verbs, which were therefore attracted into the second position.

phrase treated in the preceding section. The normal word order is: SUBJECT — *BE* — COMPLEMENT; a frequently found variation of this order was: *BE* — SUBJECT — COMPLEMENT. (*BE* stands here for any substantive verb). The following examples are taken from the *Chronicle*:

> 7 Miercne wurdon Cristne (*Chronicle* 655 A.D.)
> 'and the Mercians became Christians'
>
> Ceolwald was Cynegilses broþur (*Chronicle* 688 A.D.)
> 'Ceolwald was Cynegilses' brother'
>
> Þonne was se Ine Cenreding (*Chronicle* 688 A.D.)
> 'Now this Ine was the son of Cenred'

Like other verbs, *to be* and *to become* are often found at the end of their clause in the older Germanic dialects when the clause is subordinate.[29] In Old English, for example, we find:

> Hamtun scire se dæl se hiere behinon sæ was (*Chronicle* 878 A.D.)
> 'that part of Hampshire which was behind the sea'

But verbs such as Old English *nemnan* 'to name, call' are almost invariably followed by the complement, even in subordinate clauses. Examples are:

> on þa stowe þe is genemned Cymenes Ora (*Chronicle* 477 A.D.)
> 'on the heath which is called Cymen's Ore'
>
> þær mon nu nemneþ Cerdices Ford (*Chronicle* 519 A.D.)
> 'at the place which they now call Cedric's Ford'
>
> in þam stede þe mon nemneþ Feþan leag (*Chronicle* 584 A.D.)
> 'in the place which they call Fethley'
>
> se steorra þe mon on boc læden hæt cometa (*Chronicle* 892 A.D.)
> 'that star which in the Latin language is called 'cometa''
>
>   the hetan uuas
> Herodes aftar is eldiron (*Heliand* 2704-5)
> 'who was called Herod, after his parent'
>
> ...Franci, tie uuir nu heizen Charlinga[30]
> 'the Franks, whom we now call Carolingians'

In one example from Gothic, the complement is not in a relative clause, but the order COMPLEMENT — *haitan* was felt by the translator to be sufficiently unnatural to justify a departure from the Greek word-order:

> þannu þan at libandin abin haitada horinondei (*Romans* I, 7, 3)
> ἄρα οὖν ζοῦντος τοῦ ἀνδρὸς μοιχαλὶς χρηματίσει
> 'but while her husband is living she is called adulterous'

(I have found no other examples in which the order of the complement and *haitan* differ from that of the Greek. The above example is not conclusive, because it could also represent a Germanic verb-second clause of the type: ADVERB — VERB.) In Old Norse no such consistency of word-order is found. The orders *hét* — COMPLEMENT and COMPLEMENT — *hét* are about equally common, e.g.:

[29] Cf. p. 55.
[30] Braune, *Lesebuch*, p. 62.

prest, þann es hét Þangbrandr (*Libellus Islandorum*)[31]
'a priest who was called Thangbrand'

prestr sá es Þormoþr hét (*Libellus Islandorum*)[32]
'a priest called Thormoth'

Yet a possibly related phenomenon, the consistent position of a name before the verb of naming in main clauses, is frequent, and has parallels elsewhere in Germanic:

Aþalsteinn hét þá konungr í Englande (*Heimskringla* 38)[33]
'the name of the king in England then was Athalsteinn'

Tryggue hét sonr Óláfs (*Heimskringla* 41)[34]
'Olaf's son was called Tryggve'

Suartr hét maþr (*Njals Saga*)[35]
'the man's name was Swart'

The word-order of Old Norse is stylistically freer than that of other Germanic dialects, and the head position of a name could be ascribed to the focus placed upon a name mentioned for the first time. There are however no counter-examples of the type *konungr hét Oláfr = 'the king's name is Olaf', for this pattern is reserved for the sense 'there was a king called Olaf'. The other Germanic dialects also have a similar normal ordering NAME — IS CALLED, e.g.:

Maria uuas siu heten (*Heliand* 252b)
'she was called Mary'

Gabriel bium ic hetan (*Heliand* 120)
'I am called Gabriel'

Zacharias uuas hie hetan (*Heliand* 76)
'he was called Zacharias'

Simeon uuas he hetan (*Heliand* 468)
'his name was Simon'

Anna uuas siu hetan (*Heliand* 504)
'she was called Anna'

þone on gear-dagum Grendel nemdon
fold-buende (*Beowulf* 1306)
'whom in days of yore earthlings named Grendel'

3. *Adverbial and other Prepositional Phrases*

a. *Remarks on Pronominal Adverbials*

The largest group of pronominal adverbials in Germanic is that formed from the Indo-European pronominal stem *t-. The group is represented by short adverbs such as:

---

[31] Heusler, *Elementarbuch*, p. 192.
[32] Heusler, *Elementarbuch*, p. 193.
[33] Heusler, *Elementarbuch*, p. 204.
[34] Heusler, *Elementarbuch*, p. 206.
[35] Heusler, *Elementarbuch*, p. 211.

> Gothic: *þan, þar, þaþro*;
> Old Saxon: *than, thar, thoh, tho*;
> Old English: *þa, þaer, þeah*;
> Old Norse: *þa, þar, þo*

The pronominal adverbs resemble other pronouns and particles in being placed at or near the front of the sentence; often, indeed, it is not possible to distinguish between a particle and an adverb, i.e., between an adverbial and a purely syntactic (connective) use of the same word. If a pronominal adverb stood in the same clause as a pronoun, however, it followed the pronoun, whereas a particle would precede the pronoun:

> 7 hie þeah þa ceastre aweredon (*Chronicle* 885 A.D.)
> 'and yet they defended the camp'
>
> 7 þær þa Deniscon sige namon (*Chronicle* 871 A.D.)
> 'and there the Danes won a victory'
>
> þær æt hyðe stod hringed-stefna (*Beowulf* 32)
> 'there at the landing-place stood the ringed ship'
>
> ne þær nænig wihta wenan þorfte
> beorhtre bote to banan folmum (*Beowulf* 158-59)
> 'there no man could hope for a lighter penalty at the murderer's hands'
>
> Uuas im thoh an sorgun hugi (*Heliand* 85)
> 'Yet his thoughts were sorrowful'
>
>   endi uundrodun alla
> bihuui he thar so lango lofsalig man,
> suuiðo frod gumo fraon sinun
> thionon thorfti, so thar er enig thegno ni deda,
> than sie thar at them uuiha uualdendes geld
> folmon frumidun. (*Heliand* 175-80)
> '...and all wondered why he so long there had cause to pray to his Lord, the praiseworthy and virtuous man, as there no man ever did before, while they were making with their hands God's sacrifice at the temple'

In these examples, we find pronominal adverbs most frequently clustered with pronouns and particles at the head of the sentence. If, however, several such light sentence elements occur in the same clause, the light adverb tends to be placed after both particles and pronouns; and if an enclitic (sentence-second) verb is present, the light adverb also follows the verb. Yet there are enough counter-examples that these statements about the position of the light adverb may not be said to represent more than a tendency. The only consistent positional feature of the light adverb is its occurrence near the beginning of the sentence together with the other light elements.

b. *Locatives and Time Adverbials*

These elements tend to occupy an interior position in the clause, but focus presumably played an important role in determining their syntax. An adverb of time was often used as a 'theme' to introduce new material into a clause:

7 þy ilcan geare Æþelstan cyning 7 Ealchere dux
micelne here ofslogon æt Sondwic on Cent (*Chronicle* 851 A.D.)
'and the same year King Æthelstan and Alderman Ealchere defeated a large army at
Sandwich in Kent'

7 þy ilcan geare hie sældon anum unwisum cyninges
þegne Miercna rice to haldanne (*Chronicle* 874 A.D.)
'and the same year they gave the kingdom of Mercia to a foolish servant of the king to rule'

þa on þære seofoð wiecan ofer Eastron he gerad to
Ecgbryhtes stane be eastan Seal wyda (*Chronicle* 878 A.D.)
'then on the seventh week after Easter he journeyed to Egbertsstone east of Salwood'

On the other hand, an adverb of place could follow a 'final' verb if the locative was
of less compelling interest than the action of the sentence. Such 'trailing' locatives
have also been described in otherwise verb-final sentences in Sanskrit; these are
what Gonda has called "amplified sentences".[36] They could therefore be an Indo-
European type. Examples are found in both Old English and Old Saxon:

Her Cynegils 7 Cuichelm gefuhton on Bean dune (*Chronicle* 614 A.D.)
'In this year Cynegils and Cuichelm fought at Benedown'

7 he þær wunade oþ þæt hiene an swan ofstang æt Pryfetes flodan (*Chronicle* 755 A.D.)
'and he remained there until a herdsman stabbed him at Priffet's Flood'

so uuit giu so managan dag
uuarun an thesero uueroldi (*Heliand* 156-57)
'since we two have been together for such a long time on this world'

c. *Directional Complements*

In verb-final clauses, directional complements immediately precede the verb of motion
which they complete:

þæt hie hrædlice of his rice foren (*Chronicle* 876 A.D.)
'that they quickly drove them from the kingdom'

7 he lytle werede unieþelice æfter wudum for (*Chronicle* 878 A.D.)
'and he, with a small band of men, made his way with difficulty to the forest'

If the verb is shifted out of its final position, the directional complement usually
remains in its original place. The pattern exemplified by the following examples thus
provides an interesting confirmation of the primacy of the clause-final verb:

7 þy ilcan dæge rad Æþelmund aldor man of Hwiecum ofer æt Cynemæres forda
(*Chronicle* 800 A.D.)
'and the same day Alderman Ethelmund rode from Wick all the way to Cynemere's Ford'

7 Healfdene for mid sumum þam here on Norþ Hymbre (*Chronicle* 875 A.D.)
'and Healfdene went with part of the army to Northumbria'

Some of the adverbial particles (preverbs) have syntactic properties which resemble
the directional complements, and are in fact probably not to be separated from them;
for example:

[36] Gonda, *Veda*; Watkins, "Sentence Structure":1041-42. A similar pattern is described in Greek
inscriptions by Kieckers (*Die Stellung*, pp. 44-45).

7 æghwæþer oþerne oftrædlice ut dræfde (*Chronicle* 877 A.D.)
'and they frequently drove one another out'

When a preverb such as *ut* is expanded by an explicit complement, the complement follows the preverb:

ær hie ut of þam geweorce foron (*Chronicle* 896 A.D.)
'before they came out of the fort'

If a parallellism is assumed between preverbs such as *ut* and other directional complements, the word order in such sentences is susceptible of an explanation by Behaghel's *Gesetz der wachsenden Glieder*, the rule which adjusts the order of surface constituents so that the shorter ones precede the longer ones.[37] This shift is also coordinate with the trend for preverbs to be placed in a pre-nominal position, a trend which had not been completed at the time of the earliest Germanic monuments.

C. CONCLUSIONS

In the preceding chapter, I have suggested that the basic constituent order which must be reconstructed for Proto-Germanic was SUBJECT — OBJECT — VERB. Certain features of the syntax of nominal constituents support the hypothesis of an earlier *SOV* language drifting in historical times toward the *SVO* type characteristic of the modern Germanic languages.[38]

The order GENITIVE — NOUN appears to be fundamental to languages of the *SOV* type, and although the order NOUN — GENITIVE (*NG*) is found in all of the older Germanic dialects, it is very rare in Old Saxon and Old English. The order *GN* found in secondary compounds in Gothic and Old Norse, and the order of the elements of the patronymics and of place names in all of the dialects makes it practically certain that GN was the original order in Proto-Germanic. The inflected genitive precedes the noun in Modern English and the Scandinavian languages, and the following genitive in German (*die Uniform des Briefträgers*) is a construction of relatively recent date. The position of the descriptive adjective in relation to the noun also appears on balance to have been ADJECTIVE — NOUN (*AN*). The following adjective was more similar to an appositional noun, but especially in Old Norse, descriptive adjectives could be attracted into the position of the appositional adjective, especially as the basic order *SOV* was given up except for a few traces.

The appositional noun followed the head noun, and this pattern runs against the expected typological ordering. Yet most of the examples cited are either titles or geographical names, which appear not to follow the same rules as proper appositions.

---

[37]   Otto Behaghel, "Beziehungen zwischen Umfang und Reihenfolge von Satzliederen", *IF* 25 (1909): 110-42. Cf. also Hirt, *Urgermanisch*, vol. III, pp. 209-10.
[38]   The following remarks concerning constituent order in Germanic from a typological point of view have as their basis the work of Greenberg, ed., *Universals*, pp. 73-113 on universals of word order.

In *SOV* languages, for example, titles regularly follow the proper name, cf. Hindi *Warmā-ji* 'Mr. Warma', Japanese *Tanaka-san* 'Mr. Tanaka', etc.[39] The order TITLE — NAME on the other hand is characteristic of *SVO/VSO* languages, cf. Indonesian *Saudara Supomo* 'Mr. Supomo' and the Western European custom generally. Old English titles such as *cyning*, *arcebiskop*, etc., retain an archaism in this respect. Significantly, in the *Chronicle* later portions often reverse the order of name and title, e.g., *Bisceop Afelwold* (*Chronicle* 984 A.D.), *se arcebisceop Landfranc* (*Chronicle* 1070 A.D.). The order of geographical name and topographical feature is also apparently *NT* in *SOV* languages, *TN* in other types, cf. Japanese *Fuji-yama* (*yama* = 'mountain'), *Hiro-shima* (*shima* = 'island'). In Modern English, the order *TN* is often found when the topographical feature is derived from French, and interesting contrasts (familiar to students of place-names) exist such as Manhattan Island *vs.* the Isle of Wight; Gallows Hill *vs.* Mount Rushmore; and other examples. The influence of Romance vernaculars would seem to be an obvious place to look for the origins of the change to *SVO* word order in West Germanic, and would also explain the longer resistance of English to this shift.

Two other expected concomitant features of *SOV* languages are, however, missing from the West Germanic dialects. Postpositions are found only in traces, such as the examples already discussed (p. 41). If they are a survival from Proto-Germanic, the prevalence of postpositions in Old Norse, especially in early verse, is somewhat puzzling, but not nearly as puzzling as the opposite assumption of a later development of postpositions from original prepositions. It seems safest to assume that post-positions did indeed continue to exist in Old Norse in spite of the more pronounced drift toward *SVO* word order.

The remarks concerning postpositions apply also to the order of the elements of the expression of comparison. In Old Norse, the 'standard' (in the dative) regularly precedes the adjective, e.g., *hverjum manni betr* 'better than any man', etc.[40] The order STANDARD — (MARKER) — ADJECTIVE is typical of *SOV* languages, whereas other types have *A-M-S*. Here again, Old Norse appears to have preserved an archaism which has been lost in the other Germanic dialects. The *Hildebrandslied* offers a unique example in West Germanic:

> dat du neo dana halt mit sus sippan man
> dinc ni gileitos (*Hildebrandslied* I.31).
> 'that you never before (?) fought a kinsman'

if *dana halt* is construed as a comparative 'before this'. The parallel with the Latin ablative of comparison and the Greek genitive of comparison is noted by Löfstedt.[41]

If a distinction is made between the 'rigid' type of SOV language and the 'flexible' type, there seems to be no doubt that Proto-Germanic must be assigned to the flexible

---

[39] This fact was first pointed out in Bach, "Amharic".
[40] Heusler, *Elementarbuch*, p. 114.
[41] Einar Löfstedt, *Syntactica: Studien und Beiträge zur Historischen Syntax des Latiens. Erster Teil: Über einige Grundfragen der Lateinischen Nominalsyntax* (Lund, Gleerup, 1942), pp. 326-28.

sub-type. Some kinds of adverbial phrases could always follow the verb, and the order of elements was subject to stylistic factors. Yet the nominal phrase in Germanic has all the hall-marks of a typical *SOV* language, and the order of surface constituents involving the verb seems to support this conclusion.

V

PROTO-GERMANIC SENTENCE-TYPES

In the preceding chapters I have been discussing the syntax of the various sentence constituents in Proto-Indo-European and the Germanic dialects and attempting to establish positional constants for these elements in Proto-Germanic. In the present chapter I will combine the sentence elements whose syntax has been discussed into hypothetical Proto-Germanic sentence-types.

Up to now my procedure has been to fit the sentence constituents into the framework of a basic clause centered around a finite verb and containing a subject (whether explicit or implicit). Not all Proto-Germanic sentences, however, contained both a subject and a verb. Brugmann, in his *Syntax des einfachen Satzes im Indogermanischen*, like most other investigators of comparative syntax, treats clause-types in which a finite verb was not present (verbless clauses) and clause-types in which a subject was not present (and not implied). For the sake of completeness in the characterization of the Proto-Germanic sentence, I will also include these clause-types in this discussion.

A. SECTION I: VERBLESS CLAUSES

1. *Interjections and Vocatives*

Under this heading I will discuss 'extra-syntactic' utterances. This type of utterance either stands alone, forming a clause in isolation from other clauses, or it is incorporated into a clause as a grammatically isolated entity.

In the older Germanic dialects both interjections and vocatives are frequently found incorporated into the structure of the clause. I have referred above to the syntax of the West Germanic exclamatory particle *hwat*; this particle often introduces a sequence-initial clause, and always forms a syntactic unit with the first word of the clause. In Old English there was an exclamatory particle *la* which, if placed within a clause, was always enclitically attached to the first word of the clause; I cite two examples:

> þæt, la, mæg secgan se þe seð ond riht
> fremeð on folce (*Beowulf* 1700)
> 'Ah, he may say that who practices truth and right among people'
>
> þæt, la, mæg secgan se ðe wyle soð specan (*Beowulf* 2846)
> 'Ah, he may say that who would tell the truth'

Such incorporated interjections, however, are not easily separated from emphatic particles.

Schwentner has presented and discussed several other interjections which have cognates and syntactic parallels elsewhere in Indo-European.[1] For example, like their Latin cognate *vae*, Gothic *wai*, Old English *wa*, *wae*, Old High German *wa* and Old Saxon *wa* are usually followed by a dative of person, e.g., Gothic *wai þus Kaurazein* οὐαί σοι χοραζείν, 'Alas for you, Chorazin!' (Matthew 11, 21). cf. Latin *vae victis* 'woe to the conquered' (Livy V).

The vocative in Proto-Indo-European was unaccented if within a clause, but accented if it was outside the clause.[2] The unaccented vocative behaved syntactically like an enclitic, in that it appeared after the first accented word of the clause. In the Germanic dialects the second position is found, but by no means consistently, e.g.:

> þui, herra, at hann þá at mér (*Morkinskinna*)[3]
> 'by receiving me well, sir'
>
> En þer, Auþon, kann ek slika þokk, sem þu gefer mer
> alt dyret (*Morkinskinna*)[4]
> 'But you, Authon, I thank as if you had given me the whole bear'
>
> meaht ðu, min wine, mece gecnawan (*Beowulf* 2047)
> 'you, my friend, might know this dagger'

The weaker stress of the vocative, however, is apparent from the rarity with which vocatives are found in the key alliteration in Germanic alliterative verse, and presumably reflects the accentual contrast in Proto-Indo-European. In the following examples (from *Beowulf*) the vocative either does not alliterate at all, or, if it does, it carries only secondary alliteration:

> þeoden Hroðgar, þæt ic þe sohte (*Beowulf* 416)
> '...prince Hrothgar, that I should seek you'
>
>   þu on selum wes,
> gold-wine gumena, ond to Geatum spræc (*Beowulf* 1170)
> 'remain in happiness, gold-friend of men, and speak to the Goths'
>
> Aris, rices weard, uton hraþe feran (*Beowulf* 1390)
> 'Arise, guardian of the realm, let us quickly go'
>
>   ne ðu him wearne geteoh
> ðinra gegncwida, glædman Hroðgar! (*Beowulf* 366-67)
> 'do not make refusal of your conversation, gracious Hrothgar!'

---

[1] Ernst Schwentner, *Interjectionen*, 24-25, *et passim*.
[2] Delbrück, *Vergleichende Syntax*, vol. III, pp. 86-88.
[3] Heusler, *Elementarbuch*, p. 204.
[4] Heusler, *Elementarbuch*, p. 204.

Where the vocative carries the key alliteration, it is always a phrase long enough to comprise the entire half-line:

> For (g)ewy(r)htum þu, wine min Beowulf
> ond for arstafum usic sohtest (*Beowulf* 457-58)
> 'You visited us, my friend Beowulf, for chance of performing deeds and for favors'

In such vocative phrases a proper name rarely alliterates.[5] Accented vocatives preceding another clause are rare in the old Germanic dialects. Behaghel points out that the Old High German translations of Latin material avoid placing a vocative before a clause, and either put it within the clause or paraphrase it into a clause with a verb; he ascribes the later practice of allowing a vocative to precede a clause to Latin influence.[6]

2. *Omission of Verb*

Omission of the copulative verb *to be*, which was common in Proto-Indo-European,[7] was possible in Proto-Germanic, but was becoming less frequent. In Gothic we find instances of the verb *wesan* introduced in a copulative equation against the Greek original, e.g.:

> þata auk ist wilja gudis
> τοῦτο γὰρ θέλημα θεοῦ
> 'for that is the will of God' (*Thessalonians* I, 5, 18)

But there are several occurrences of the verbal compound *kara wesan* 'to be of concern' in which the inflected part of *wesan* is omitted even when *kara ist* corresponds to a Greek finite verb (μέλει), e.g.:

> niu kara þuk þizei fraqistnam (*Mark*, 4, 38)
> οὐ μέλει σοι ὅτι ἀπολλύμεθα,
> 'don't you care about our destruction?'

In all occurrences of *kara* without *wesan*, the verb would be in the present indicative; the following optative form:

> ni þeei ina þize þarbane kara wesi (*John* 12, 6)
> οὐχ ὅτι περι τῶν πτωχῶν ἔμελεν αὐτῷ
> 'not because he was concerned about the poor'

makes it reasonable to suppose that *wesan* could be omitted with *kara* if it was present indicative, i.e., if it was in the 'unmarked' form of the paradigm. The only other Germanic monuments which give evidence that omission of the copulative verb was less than rare in Proto-Germanic are the Runic inscriptions, which, however, present so many problems of interpretation that one is wary of drawing conclusions based

---

[5] Cf. Lehmann, *Old Saxon Poetry*, p. 34. Lehmann notes that in the *Heliand* and in other alliterative verse, proper names in general are rare in the key alliteration, and attributes it to the fact that names limit rather than describe; "limiting forms were apparently relatively weakly stressed".
[6] Behagel, *Deutsche Syntax*, vol. IV, p. 253.
[7] Brugmann, *Die Syntax*, p. 59.

on them. Especially omission of the verb *to be* could be an inscriptional convention which did not correspond to contemporary usage. In the Runic materials I find the following examples:

> ek hagustaldaR þewaR godagas (*Valsfjord Rock Inscription*)[8]
> 'I (am) a warrior, follower of Godag'
>
> ek irilaR wiwila (*Veblungsnes Rock Inscription*)[9]
> 'I (am) the Rune-master Wiwila'

These three inscriptions are all old (Krause suggests 400 A. D., 550 A. D., and 400 A. D. respectively). Brugmann states [10] that omission of the copulative verb was especially common in Proto-Indo-European under two conditions. One was when the verb was present indicative and in the third person; the use of Gothic *kara wesan* corresponds to this condition. The second condition was when the subject of the clause was first or second person personal pronoun; again, we see this situation in the Runic examples above, where the subject is *ek* 'I'.

In all the Germanic dialects a non-finite verb of motion could be omitted if the direction and mode of action were irrelevant or evident from the context. An especially frequent instance is when a directional complement or a preverb and a modal auxiliary occur in the clause, e.g.:

> þær him mon to ne meahte (*Chronicle* 877 A.D.)
> 'where no one could reach him'

B. SECTION II: SUBJECTLESS SENTENCES

I exclude from the subjectless sentences those sentences in which the subject is present but not expressed, as, for example, Old Saxon *quað* 'he said' (e.g., *Heliand* 2050). I also exclude imperative sentences, with less certainty, but chiefly on the grounds that the subject of an imperative *can* be expressed and in the older Germanic dialects often was, e.g., Old English *ne beo ðu ne forth* 'be thou not afraid' (*Andreas* 98).

The most commonly encountered types of subjectless clauses are those describing natural phenomena and those expressing a subjective state. The two types are represented by the Gothic *rigneiþ* 'it rains' (*Matthew* 5, 45) and **mik huggreiþ* 'I hunger' (cf. *John* 6, 35 *þana gaggandan du mis ni huggreiþ* ὥ ἐρχόμενος πρός με οὐ μὴ πεινάσῃ ' he who comes to me shall not hunger'). Both types are reconstructable for Proto-Indo-European.[11] In Proto-Germanic as in Proto-Indo-European no expletive (*Scheinsubjekt*) was used; the development of a pseudo-subject (German *es regnet*,

[8]   Krause, *Die Runeninschriften*, p. 123.
[9]   Krause, *Die Runeninschriften*, p. 116.
[10] Brugmann, *Die Syntax*, 59.
[11] Cf. Brugmann, *Die Syntax*, pp. 17-41; Hirt, *Grammatik*, vol. VII, pp. 8-22. The bibliography of subjectless sentences in Indo-European and Germanic is extensive. In the present study I can do little more than merely indicate that Proto-Germanic possessed the same kinds of subjectless sentences as Proto-Indo-European, with some modifications.

French *il pleut*) belongs to the history of the individual Germanic and Romance dialects.

The other impersonal constructions in the Germanic dialects can be divided into two groups. One group consists of verbs which are not normally impersonal, but whose subject is too vague to be specified. This type is, I believe, peculiar to the North Germanic dialects in historical times; in the West Germanic dialects we find a pronoun (e.g., Old English *mon*) in the role of subject. In the North Germanic dialects we have examples such as the following:

> Opt sparir leiðom þatz hefir ljúfom hugat[12] (*Hávamál* 40)
> 'one often saves for one's enemies that which one had thought up for one's friends'
>
> sva skal vittni bæra: bær iak þæs vittni[13]
> 'this is how one (formally) bears witness: 'I bear witness thereto'' (Old Swedish laws)
>
> vatn skal eigh vænda af fornu fari
> 'no one shall divert water from its previous course'[14]

The development of a special personal pronoun in the West Germanic dialects is late, for the pronoun used, *man*, is etymologically identical with the word *man*, 'vir, homo'. Furthermore, there is some indication that in Old English the pronoun *mon* was very closely linked syntactically to the verb, for in the Old English of the *Chronicle*, *mon* is with only one or two exceptions always in direct contact with the verb, even when normal order SUBJECT — OBJECT — VERB and, *a fortiori*, PRONOUN — NOUN — VERB is violated. Examples are:

> 7 Hæstenes wif 7 his suna twegen mon brohte to þæm cyning (*Chronicle* 894 A.D.)
> 'and they brought Haesten's wife and two sons to the king'
>
> 7 hiene mon þær ofslog (*Chronicle* 878 A.D.)
> 'and there they killed him'

In Proto-Germanic the unspecified subject construction was formed by omitting the subject altogether. Whether the verb was in the active voice, as in North Germanic, or whether it continued to use the middle voice (cf. Latin *itur* '*on va*'), is difficult to say. The periphrastic passive is found in the West Germanic dialects (cf. Modern German *es wird gesungen*) and in Gothic (*gameliþ ist* 'γέγραπται''); according to Brugmann, the use of the middle to express an unspecified subject is found in the Gothic *atsteiga-dau* 'καταβάτω', in the sense 'let there be a descending' *qu'on descende*), but there seem to be few further examples of the construction with the middle voice.[15]

Like the other Indo-European languages, Proto-Germanic contained a number of verbs whose 'logical' subject was expressed indirectly. Examples of such verbs in Gothic are:

> bajoþum gabairgada (*Matthew* 9, 17)
> ἀμφότεροι συνηροῦνται
> 'both shall be preserved (to-both it-shall-be-preserved)'

12 From Neckel, *Edda*.
13 From Delbrück, *Syntax IV*, p. 11.
14 From Delbrück, *Syntax IV*, p. 6.
15 Cf. discussion in Brugmann, *Syntax des Einfachen Satzes* pp. 39-40.

þei waihtai ni fraqistnai (*John* 6, 12)

ἵνα μή τι ἀπόληται

'that none should spoil (that to-one it-should-get-spoilt)'

ni þeei ina þize þarbane kara wesi (*John* 12, 6)

οὐχ ὅτι περὶ τῶν πτωχῶν ἔμελεν αὐτῷ

'not because he was concerned (concern was to him) about the needy'

Within the framework of the present study I can do no more than point to the existence of subjectless sentences of this type, for they present problems of verb and case morphology rather than of syntax.

C. SECTION III: BASIC PROTO-GERMANIC SENTENCE TYPES

I will now give a schematic outline of the most fundamental characteristics of the Proto-Germanic sentence.

Bloomfield distinguished four ways of arranging linguistic forms:[16]

1. Order: the succession in which the constituents of a complex form are spoken;
2. Modulation: the use of secondary (suprasegmental) phonemes;
3. Phonetic modification: (morphophonemic or phonotactic) change in the primary phonemes of a form;
4. Selection of forms.

In this section, as in the whole of this study, I will be concerned mainly with the first of these, order, and will not deal at all with the third and fourth. I will, however, discuss briefly the possibility of reconstructing the modulation of the Proto-Germanic sentence.

1. *Order*

a. *The Neutral Word Order*

Under this heading I will consider clauses which do not serve a special function, and which are not intended to have an emphatic or unusual effect.

The most basic clause-type of all in Proto-Germanic, and the one from which other types are derived in the simplest and most easily accountable way, is that in which the finite verb is placed at the end of the clause, and the other constituents occur in the order indicated here. Schematically, this basic clause consists of the following constituents in order:

⧣ PARTICLES — PRONOUNS — PRONOMINAL ADVEBS — SUBJECT NOMINAL —
INDIRECT OBJECT NOMINAL
⎱   — DIRECT OBJECT NOMINAL — HEAVY ADVERBS —
NOMINAL COMPLEMENT
VERBAL COMPLEX ⧣

[16]   Leonard Bloomfield, *Language* (Chicago, Holt, 1933), pp. 163-64.

The constituents could be expanded into elements ordered as follows:

Nominal: POSSESSIVE
                    — DESCRIPTIVE ADJECTIVE —
       DEMONSTRATIVE

                APPOSITIONAL ADJECTIVE
       NOUN —
                ONAL NOUNAPPOSITI

                      DIRECTIONAL COMPLEMENT
Adverb: NON-PRONOMINAL ADVERB —
                      ADVERBIAL PHRASE

Verbal Complex: REFLEXIVE — PREVERB — NON-FINITE VERB — NEGATION —
                FINITE VERB

The 'ideal' word order represented by this schema was frequently disrupted by stylistic, functional and rhythmical factors. The heavy adverbial elements were especially susceptible of syntactic change. In the North Germanic dialects and Gothic, the possessive and the demonstrative have taken on the possibility of appearing after rather than before the nominal.

I shall now give a number of examples illustrating the order of elements in the neutral, verb-final clause. We do not expect to find one sentence containing all the elements described, of course, and I therefore give several clauses which have these elements in close agreement with the schema. No statistical support is offered for the frequency of the types represented by each example, but on the other hand I have attempted to take examples from contexts which are as near as I can judge stylistically unmarked. The value of the examples is reduced by their restriction to West Germanic dialects, for verb-final clauses in North Germanic are so rare as to be inconclusive. Yet the Old Norse evidence need not be ignored, for, as I will show later, the neutral word-order in Old Norse is also derived from the basic clause-type surmised above for Proto-Germanic.

(1) *Old English*

> 7 se here þa burg be seten hæfde (*Chronicle* 894 A.D.)
> 'and the army had besieged the city'

Type: # PARTICLE — SUBJECT NOMINAL — DIRECT OBJECT NOMINAL — (PREVERB) NON-FINITE VERB — FINITE VERB #

> (he þone dæg forlure) þe he noht to gode on ne gedyde (*Chronicle* 81 A.D.)
> '(that day was lost to him) on which he did nothing good'

Type: # PARTICLE — PRONOUN — DIRECT OBJECT NOMINAL — ADVERB — PREVERB — NEGATION — FINITE VERB #

> 7 hie him friþ wiþ namon (*Chronicle* 866 A.D.)
> 'and they made peace with them'

Type: # PARTICLE — PRONOUN[1] — PRONOUN[2] — DIRECT OBJECT NOMINAL — PREVERB — VERB #

7 hie be him lifgendum hie gedældon (*Chronicle* 718 A.D.)
'and they parted from one another during their lifetime'

Type: # PARTICLE — PRONOUN — ADVERBIAL PHRASE — REFLEXIVE — FINITE VERB #

7 æghwæþer oþerne oftrædlice ut dræfde (*Chronicle* 877 A.D.)
'and each drove out the other frequently'

Type: # PARTICLE — SUBJECT NOMINAL — DIRECT OBJECT NOMINAL — (POLYSYL-LABIC) ADVERB — PREVERB — FINITE VERB #

þæt hie hrædlice of his rice foren (*Chronicle* 876 A.D.)
'that they would leave his kingdom immediately'

Type: # PARTICLE — PRONOUN — POLYSYLLABIC ADVERB — DIRECTIONAL COMPLE-MENT — FINITE VERB #

7 hie þeah micle fierd gegadrodon (*Chronicle* 867 A.D.)
'and they nonetheless gathered a large force'

Type: # PARTICLE — PRONOUN — PRONOMINAL ADVERB — DIRECT OBJECT NOMINAL — FINITE VERB #

(2) *Old Saxon*

that ic bi thiu an thesa uuerold quami (*Heliand* 1420)
'that this is why I came to this world'

Type: # PARTICLE — PRONOUN — HEAVY ADVERB — DIRECTIONAL COMPLEMENT — FINITE VERB #

ef gi im thus fulgangan uuillead (*Heliand* 1689)
'if you thus take thought for him'

Type: # PARTICLE — PRONOUN — PRONOMINAL ADVERB — NON-FINITE VERB — FINITE VERB #

Tho it im at themu endie ni dugie (*Heliand* 1780)
'Though it will not profit him at the end'

Type: # PARTICLE — PRONOUN[1] — PRONOUN[2] — ADVERBIAL PHRASE — NEGATION — FINITE VERB #

er it im the helago Crist
obar that erlo folc oponum uuordum
thurh is selbes craft seggean welda (*Heliand* 2372-74)
'before holy Christ told it by his own authority to them with open words amongst the good people'

Type: # PARTICLE — PRONOUN[1] — PRONOUN[2] — SUBJECT NOMINAL — HEAVY ADVERBS (1-3) — NON-FINITE VERB — FINITE VERB #

that he sie gerno forð
lestien uuillie (*Heliand* 2498)
'that he might want to carry out (the words)'

Type: # PARTICLE — PRONOUN[1] — PRONOUN[2] — ADVERB — PREVERB — NON-FINITE VERB — FINITE VERB #

(3) *Old High German*

>dat ih dir it nu bi huldi gibu (*Hildebrandslied* 35)
>'this I now give to you out of friendship'

Type: # PRONOUNS (1-4) — PRONOMINAL ADVERB — HEAVY ADVERB — FINITE
VERB #

>daz er kotes uuillun kerno tuo (*Muspilli* 20)
>'that he is willing to do God's will'

Type: # PARTICLE — PRONOUN — DIRECT OBJECT NOMINAL — HEAVY ADVERB —
FINITE VERB #

>uuanta sar so sih diu sela in den sind arhevit (*Muspilli* 2)
>'for as soon as the soul rises in that direction'

Type: # PARTICLES (1-3) — REFLEXIVE (1) — NOMINAL SUBJECT — ADVERBIAL PHRASE —
FINITE VERB #

>so dar manno nohhein uuiht pimidan ni mak (*Muspilli* 90)
>'thus no man there can in any way avoid it'

Type: # PARTICLE — PRONOMINAL ADVERB — SUBJECT NOMINAL — HEAVY ADVERB —
NON-FINITE VERB — NEGATION — FINITE VERB #

>dar der heligo Christ ana arhangan uuard (*Muspilli* 101)
>'whereon holy Christ was crucified'

Type: # PRONOMINAL ADVERB — SUBJECT NOMINAL — PREVERB — NON-FINITE
VERB — FINITE VERB #

To discuss all the possible stylistic transformations of the basic clause in the Germanic dialects would be an undertaking beyond the scope of present study. I have mentioned some of the possible transformations already: a heavy adverb which contributed only little to the sense of the clause could be placed after the finite verb; a heavy adverb to which emphasis was attached could be placed either at the head of the clause or before the last nominal element. The transformations with which I shall be concerned affect the position of the finite verb. I will deal first with transformations which depend on the lexical and rhythmical *weight* of the verb.

In the earliest recorded Germanic dialects the finite verb was placed toward the head of the sentence with the particles and pronominal elements. The circumstances under which this transformation took place in the historical languages are not always clear, but some general statements have been made in an earlier chapter.[17] From the point of view of the syntax of the whole sentence, we find that the shift of the verb to the 'enclitic' position did not affect the syntax of the other sentence-elements, except that a non-finite verb and its preverb might be placed one position nearer the beginning of the sentence. The 'enclitic' verb of the Germanic languages can be explained by a simple transformation of part of a verbal complex from final to second

---

[17] Cf. p. 58.

(or, more generally, near-initial) position which affected only the finite verb. On the other hand, to assume that the second position was original, and to derive the final position from it, involves the considerably more complex shift of both the non-finite and finite elements of the verbal constituents. I therefore assume that the second position, and not the final position, of the verb was a later development.

I will now give examples from the early Germanic dialects in which the verb appears among the clause initial light elements. I have chosen these examples so as to avoid both 'enclisis' of the verb, which we may define as the position of a finite verb immediately following an emphatic element at the beginning of a clause, and the series-initiating clause-initial verb, as well as other clause-initial verbs in marked word-order. But the 'enclitic' verb is a result of the same transformation of the neutral word order except that a prior transformation has placed an emphatic element at the head of the clause. If the finite verb occurred at the head of the clause with the particle and pronominal elements, there appears to be no conventional ordering of particles, pronouns and verb beyond the expected ones that particles which are not enclitic are placed at the beginning of the clause, and the subject pronoun precedes the verb. Hirt assumes a basic ordering of unaccented elements in Proto-Germanic: PARTICLES — PRONOUNS — VERB — VOCATIVE,[18] but I find no evidence for this ordering and Hirt provides none.

(4) *Old Norse*

> en þá es hann hafþe hér veret einn vetr eða tvá (*Libellus Islandorum*)[19]
> 'but when he had been there one or two winters'

Type: # PARTICLES (1-3) — PRONOUN — (FINITE VERB) — ADVERB[1] — (NON-FINITE VERB) — ADVERBIAL PHRASE #

> at hann skylde log þeira upp segia (*Libellus Islandorum*)[20]
> 'that he should expound their law'

Type: # PARTICLE — PRONOUN — (FINITE VERB) — NOMINAL DIRECT OBJECT PREVERB — NON-FINITE VERB #

> En hann lauk svá mále sino (*Libellus Islandorum*)[21]
> 'but he shut his mouth at once'

Type: # PARTICLE — PRONOUN — (FINITE VERB) — PRONOMINAL ADVERB — DIRECT OBJECT NOMINAL #

(5) *Old English*

> (her wæs se mona) swelce he wære mid blode begoten (*Chronicle* 734 A.D.)
> '(In this year the moon was) as if it had been poured over with blood'

[18] Hirt, *Handbuch*, vol. III, pp. 227-28.
[19] Gordon, *Old Norse*, p. 36.
[20] Gordon, *Old Norse*, p. 37.
[21] Gordon, *Old Norse*, p. 38.

Type: # PARTICLE — PRONOUN — (FINITE VERB) — ADVERBIAL PHRASE — NON-
FINITE VERB #

7 he heold þone bisc:dom .xxvii. win:t on Winta ceastre (*Chronicle* 703 A.D.)
'and he held the bishopric in Winchester for 27 winters'

Type: # PARTICLE — PRONOUN — (FINITE VERB) — DIRECT OBJECT NOMINAL —
ADVERBIAL PHRASE[1] — ADVERBIAL PHRASE[2] #

forþon he wolde þone Xr:es geleafan geryhten (*Chronicle* 680 A.D.)
'because he wanted to set right the Christian faith'

Type: # PARTICLE — PRONOUN — (FINITE VERB) — DIRECT OBJECT NOMINAL —
NON-FINITE VERB #

þæt hie ne mehton þa scypu ut brengan (*Chronicle* 896 A.D.)
'that they could not get the ships out'

Type: # PARTICLE — PRONOUN — (NEGATION — FINITE VERB) — DIRECT OBJECT
NOMINAL — PREVERB — NON-FINITE VERB #

(6) *Old High German*

Ioh auh dher selbo uuardh dhurah esaian dher forasagun
chiforabodot, "qui etiam et per isaiam prophetam
ita pronuntiatur" (Isidor, *Contra Judeos*, 39, 21)
'And he himself was also foretold by the prophet Isaiah'

Type: # PARTICLES (1-2) — SUBJECT NOMINAL — (FINITE VERB) — ADVERBIAL
PHRASE — NON-FINITE VERB #

dhazs noh ni sii dhazs ziidh arfullit "(dicunt) nondum
esse hoc tempus expletum" (Isidor, *Contra Iudeos* 35, 10)
'that that time had not yet been fulfilled'

Type: # PARTICLE — PRONOMINAL ADVERB — (NEGATION — FINITE VERB) —
SUBJECT NOMINAL — NON-FINITE VERB #

(7) *Old Saxon*

so man herren scal
gerno fulgangan (*Heliand* 110-11)
'as one should willingly follow the Lord'

Type: # PARTICLE — PRONOUN — DIRECT OBJECT NOMINAL — (FINITE VERB) —
HEAVY ADVERB — NON-FINITE VERB #

the sprac im mid is uuordun to (*Heliand* 114)
'who addressed him with these words'

Type: # PARTICLE/PRONOUN — (FINITE VERB) — PRONOUN — ADVERBIAL PHRASE —
PREVERB #

he ni mohte tho enig uuord sprekan (*Heliand* 184)
'he was unable to speak a single word'

Type: # PRONOUN — (NEGATION — FINITE VERB) — PRONOMINAL ADVERB —
DIRECT OBJECT NOMINAL — NON-FINITE VERB #

> Huuat thu huuargin ni tharft
> mid thinun fotun an felis bespurnan (*Heliand* 1089-90)
> 'In no way would you have cause to dash your feet against the rock'

Type: # PARTICLE — PRONOUN — PRONOMINAL ADVERB — (NEGATION — FINITE VERB) — ADVERBIAL PHRASES (1-2) — NON-FINITE VERB #

b. *The Marked Word-Order*

The clause whose finite verb was stressed and placed at the initial position served in Proto-Germanic to introduce a series of clauses, or to perform a specialized function such as imperative, interrogative and conditional.[22] The syntax of the other constituents in verb-initial clauses is less consistent than that of verb-second and verb-final clauses; the verb-initial clause almost always has a special stylistic motivation, and the order of elements is for the most part unpredictable. I have observed the following general patterns, however: if the subject of the verb is a nominal and the clause contains light elements, the light elements intervene between the verb and the subject; and if the subject is a pronoun, it immediately follows the verb. If a verb-initial clause contains both heavy adverbs and a nominal subject, the subject may be given special emphasis by being placed AFTER the adverb. If the verb is preceded by proclitic *þa*, the subject immediately follows it even if light elements are thereby shifted into a later position.[23] Examples are as follows.

(1) *Old English*

> Hylde hine tha heaþodeor (*Beowulf* 688)
> 'the warrior then laid himself down'

Type: # FINITE VERB — PRONOUN — PRONOMINAL ADVERB — NOMINAL SUBJECT #

> Gewiton him ða wigend wica neosian (*Beowulf* 1125)
> 'The warriors went to seek out their dwellings'

Type: # FINITE VERB — PRONOUN — SUBJECT NOMINAL — DIRECT OBJECT NOMINAL NON-FINITE VERB #

> Ofereode þa æþelinga bearn
> steap stanhlið (*Beowulf* 1408)
> 'Then the noble warrior passed over steep gorges'

Type: # FINITE VERB — PRONOMINAL ADVERB — SUBJECT NOMINAL — DIRECT OBJECT NOMINAL #

> þa ne mehte sio fird na hindan of faran (*Chronicle* 894 A.D)
> 'The (English) army was unable to cut off their retreat'

Type: # *þa* — NEGATION — FINITE VERB — SUBJECT NOMINAL — HEAVY ADVERB — NON-FINITE VERB #

---

[22] Cf. pp. 48-52.
[23] Yet in Old Saxon light elements are placed between VERB and SUBJECT NOMINAL even when the clause is introduced by *tho*.

Þa gemetton þa men hie of Here forda 7 of Gleawa ceastre (*Chronicle* 918 A.D.)
'the men of Hereford and Gloucester met them'

Type: # *þa* — FINITE VERB — SUBJECT NOMINAL PRONOUN — (DISCONTINUOUS COMPLEMENTS OF SUBJECT) #

With emphatic postponement of SUBJECT:

Þa com of more under misthleoþum
Grendel gongan (*Beowulf* 710-11)
'From the moor under cover of darkness Grendel came walking'

Type: # *þa* — FINITE VERB — ADVERBIAL PHRASES (1-2) — SUBJECT NOMINAL — NON-FINITE VERB #

Gewat þa ofer wægholm winde gefysed
flota famiheals (*Beowulf* 217-18)
'Driven by the wind, the foamy necked boat moved over the ocean waves'

Type: # FINITE VERB — ADVERBIAL PHRASE — (PARENTHETICAL COMPLEMENT) — SUBJECT NOMINAL #

(2) *Old Norse*

Hefer Auþon dýr sitt miþ sér (*Libellus Islandorum*)[24]
'Authon had his animal with him'

Type: # FINITE VERB — SUBJECT NOMINAL — DIRECT OBJECT NOMINAL — ADVERBIAL PHRASE #

Þa lét konungr gøra honom laug (*Libellus Islandorum*)[25]
'the king had him bathed'

Type: # *þa* — FINITE VERB — SUBJECT NOMINAL — NON-FINITE VERB — PRONOUN — DIRECT OBJECT NOMINAL #

Gaf hann mer leþrhoso fulla af silfre (*Libellus Islandorum*)[26]
'he gave me leather gaiters set with silver'

Type: # FINITE VERB — PRONOUN — PRONOUN — DIRECT OBJECT NOMINAL #

Gengr þa upp alt féet (*Libellus Islandorum*)[27]
'the money had all gone'

Type: # FINITE VERB — PRONOMINAL ADVERB — PREVERB — SUBJECT NOMINAL #

(3) *Old High German*

Garutun se iro guðhamun (*Hildebrandslied* 5)
'they put on their battle-dress'

Floh her Otachres nid (*Hildebrandslied* 18)
'he fled the wrath of Otoacer'

Type: # FINITE VERB — PRONOUN — DIRECT OBJECT NOMINAL #

---

[24] Heusler, *Elementarbuch*, p. 196.
[25] Heusler, *Elementarbuch*, p. 201.
[26] Heusler, *Elementarbuch*, p. 201.
[27] Heusler, *Elementarbuch*, p. 198.

do lettun se aerist asckim scritan (*Hildebrandslied* 63)
'first they let fly their ashen lances'

Type: # *þa*—FINITE VERB—HEAVY ADVERB—(EMPHATIC) DIRECT OBJECT NOMINAL— NON-FINITE VERB #

verit denne stuatago in land (*Muspilli* 55)
'then the day of battle moves into the land'

Type: # FINITE VERB — PRONOMINAL ADVERB — SUBJECT NOMINAL — ADVERBIAL PHRASE #

scal imo avar sin lip piqueman (*Muspilli* 82)
'his body shall be joined to him again'

Type: # FINITE VERB — PRONOUN — HEAVY ADVERB — (EMPHATIC) SUBJECT NOMINAL — NON-FINITE VERB #

(4) *Old Saxon*

Ni quam ic an thesaro uuerold ti thiu (*Heliand* 1428)
'Not for this reason did I come to this world'

Type: # NEGATION — FINITE VERB — PRONOUN — ADVERBIAL PHRASES (1-2) #

Tho sprak im iro drohtin to (*Heliand* 2925)
'their Lord addressed them'

Type: # *þa* — FINITE VERB — PRONOUN — SUBJECT NOMINAL — PREVERB #

Ne mugun gi iu betaran rad
geuuinnan an thesoro uueroldi (*Heliand* 1462-63)
'There is no better profit you could gain in this world'

Type: # NEGATION — FINITE VERB — PRONOUNS — DIRECT OBJECT NOMINAL — NON-FINITE VERB — ADVERBIAL PHRASE #

Tho giuuet imu uualdand Crist
siðon fan themu see (*Heliand* 2973-74)
'The Lord Christ went afterward away from the sea'

Type: # *þa* — FINITE VERB — PRONOUN — SUBJECT NOMINAL — ADVERBS (1-2) #

With these examples of reflexes of the basic ordering of Proto-Germanic sentence elements in the early Germanic dialects and of the simpler transformations which they could undergo, I conclude my discussion of the positional syntax of the Proto-Germanic simple sentence. I will now consider the possibility of reconstructing the stress and pitch contours which characterized the simple sentence.

2. *Modulation*

In attempting to reconstruct suprasegmental phonemes and intonation contours for Proto-Germanic, we have first to consider the interplay of stress (dynamic accent) and pitch (musical accent).

Although, from alliterative verse and from older syntactic patterns, we have evidence on which to base a reconstruction of stress contours in the sentence, we can only guess at the role of pitch. The comparative study of suprasegmentals in the Indo-European dialects has uncovered the correspondence between the musical accent of Greek and Sanskrit and the stress accent of Germanic, and has investigated the phonological consequences of this correspondence, such as Verner's Law. It is not assumed, of course, that Proto-Germanic had no secondary phonemes of pitch; it is, however, impossible with our present knowledge to reconstruct them, and there seems little prospect of being able to do so. Presumably, in Proto-Germanic some types of questions had a special musical sentence-intonation, yet we find no special treatment of question intonation in alliterative verse. In my discussion I will regard pitch in Proto-Germanic as secondary to stress, so that, for example, the term FALLING INTONATION refers not to a group of high followed by low-pitched syllables, but to a stressed element followed by more weakly stressed elements. In other words, I regard the Proto-Germanic accentual system as resembling that of the modern West Germanic dialects rather than that of Swedish or Norwegian.

I assume at least three levels of stress in the Proto-Germanic clause, according to the role of the heaviest-stressed syllable of a word in the contour of the clause. I shall not discuss the secondary phonemes below the word-level. These levels of stress were distributed as follows over the various word-classes:[28]

1. Primary stress ('): Nouns, Adjectives, Numerals, Heavy Adverbs containing a Nominal, Non-finite Verbs.
2. Secondary stress (^): Most adverbs, preverbs.
3. Weak stress (ᵕ): Particles, pronouns, pronominal adverbs, verbs, quantifiers (e.g. *all*, *many*)

In combinations, this distribution was changed. The evidence of alliterative verse suggests a number of characteristic stress-sandhi phenomena. The most important of these is that if two words of an identical word-class stood next to one another, the stress of the second one was reduced; similarly, the stress of a noun preceded by adjectives or numerals was also reduced. If a sentence-element followed another sentence-element so closely as to be in an enclitic or near-enclitic dependency, the prior element received a stronger stress and the following element might lose its stress. If the clause was introduced by a number of light (i.e., weakly-stressed) elements, the first of these elements was given a stronger stress than the following ones.

As a result of these accentual modifications, the characteristic pattern of the larger constituents in the Proto-Germanic sentence was an initial (phonetic) primary stress followed by a progressive weakening of the stress of subsequent elements, i.e., a 'falling intonation'. The stress contour of the larger constituent therefore resembled

---

[28] Cf. Max Rieger, "Die ält- und angelsächsische verskunst", *ZfdPh* 7 (1876):1-63.

the newly-developed accentuation pattern of the later Proto-Germanic word: a strong accent on the initial member with simultaneous weakening of the accent of subsequent members. In the following examples, in which the second member of a constituent does not alliterate, the assumed weaker accent is marked with the grave accent `, while the alliterating member is marked with the acute accent ´.

a. *Two Words of the Same Category in Juxtaposition*

Wiglaf maþelode, Wéohstanes sùnu (*Beowulf* 2862)
'Wiglaf, son of Weohstan, said'

Hroðgar maþelode, hélm Scỳldinga (*Beowulf* 371)
'Hrothgar, lord of the Scyldings, said'

næfre he on aldordagum ǽr ne sìþðan (*Beowulf* 718)
'never in his lifedays, before or since'

ferdon folctogon féorran and nèan (*Beowulf* 839)
'chiefs came from far and near'

b. *Noun Preceded by Adjective*

byreð blódig wæl, byrgean þenceð (*Beowulf* 448)
'carrying the bloody corpse, intending to eat it'

min ýldra mæg unlifigende (*Beowulf* 468)
'my elder kinsmen, bereft of life'

c. *Prior Element Receives Stronger Stress Because of Weakly Stressed Following Element*

(Here I include alliterating clause-initial verbs followed by *þa*, and clause-initial groups of light elements introduced by a particle such as *hwæt*.)

Gemúnde þă se goda, mæg Higelaces (*Beowulf* 758)
'Then the good man, the kinsman of Higelac, remembered'

Gewát hĭm þă waroðe wicge ridan (*Beowulf* 234)
'then he went ashore riding a horse'

Hwæt, mĕ þæs on eþle edwenden cwom (*Beowulf* 1774)
'Because of that, a change came to me in my native-land'

In Proto-Germanic the final element of a clause was usually the finite verb. In alliterative verse a final verb is almost always unstressed; it is stressed only if the other elements in the half-line are pronouns and particles, as in:

Hie þæt ne wíston, þa hie gewin drugon (*Beowulf* 798)
'They did not know, when they fought the battle'

The weakly stressed finite verb was thus involved in a falling intonation in the sentence-terminal.

At the beginning of the neutral sentence were placed the weakly-stressed elements, pronouns, particles and pronominal adverbs (but not the verb). Yet the sentence did not open with a weakly-stressed unit, but with a particle whose stress was greater than the other light elements; the opening particle may have had, phonetically, secondary stress.[29] The initial syllables of the neutral sentence would have had the intonation pattern: $\hat{x} \; \breve{x} \; \breve{x} \; \breve{x}$... Nominal elements in the sentence had the strongest, primary stress. Form the point of view of the intonation contour, the sentence centered around the nouns. The nominal groups were characterized by a falling intonation: the initial member of a group received a stronger stress than the following members.

Adverbial elements had a stress intermediate between the primary stress of the nominal elements and the weak stress of the light elements and the finite verb. An adverb did not alliterate in the presence of a noun, but took precedence over a verb, e.g.:

> eóten wæs útweard, éorl fûrþur stop (*Beowulf* 761)
> 'the monster was eager to escape, (but) the warrior moved forward'

But:

> nean ond feorran þu nú hafast (*Beowulf* 1174)
> 'near and far you now have'

A noun forming part of an adverbial phrase, however, alliterated like any other noun, e.g.:

> banfatu bærnan, ond on bǽl don (*Beowulf* 1116)
> '...to burn the body, and put upon the funeral pyre...'

There was therefore not necessarily a continually falling intonation after the subject and complement nominal elements; the secondary stress of the adverbs could be followed again by the primary stress of a noun in a prepositional phrase. There is, indeed, some evidence that the alternation of strongly and weakly stressed elements was a preferred intonation pattern. Behaghel has pointed out frequent instances in the Germanic dialects in which a shorter or more weakly stressed member of a larger constituent is placed between two longer or more strongly stressed elements.[30] In the neutral sentence in Proto-Germanic, then, I conclude that we may distinguish three colons:

1. An introductory group of weakly stressed elements, the first of which had a predictable secondary stress;
2. A series of elements with primary and secondary stress, some of which were arranged so that stronger and weaker stresses alternated;
3. A final colon having a falling intonation. The fall could be abrupt, as when a finite verb followed a noun or non-finite verb, or it could be gradual, as when the finite verb was preceded by adverbs and preverbs.

---

[29] I have in this study largely ignored the evidence offered by accented Old High German texts as being too uncertain and inconsistent to be of value. Kluge, however, points out that *unde* (the Old High German cognate of Old English *ond*) is consistently accented by Notker (Kluge, *Urgermanisch*, p. 97).
[30] Behaghel, *Deutsche Syntax*, vol. IV, pp. 6, 117, 203, 212, 233.

Among the most frequent variations of this rhythmical pattern was that in which the first stress was occupied, not by an initial particle, but by another clause-element, such as a verb, noun, preverb or adverb. Weakly stressed elements then followed the initial element in enclitic or near-enclitic dependency. An initial verb could be preceded by an unstressed proclitic particle, *þa*, whose rhythmical function was perhaps to give greater prominence to the normally unaccented finite verb.

D. SECTION IV: GENERAL CONCLUSIONS AND PREVIEW
OF FUTURE RESEARCH

The most important conclusion from the point of view of comparative Indo-European syntax is that the Germanic languages in their earliest recorded stages contained syntactic patterns similar to those of the most archaic, peripheral Indo-European dialects. Just as the Proto-Germanic phonological system can be compared in its conservatism only to that of Greek and Armenian,[31] so do its basic syntactic configurations stand beside those of Hittite, Vedic Sanskrit, and Old Irish.

A second conclusion is significant for the comparative and textual study of the Germanic dialects. It is possible to set up a fundamental neutral linear ordering of sentence-elements which may be applied to all the older dialects. Apart from a few consistent changes in individual dialects, such as the establishment of a near-initial verb in Old Norse, this fundamental ordering was largely retained in the early Germanic literary monuments. If we assume that the basic ordering of elements was as I have described it in the first four chapters and summarized in the second section of the present chapter, we must be prepared to assign a special stylistic interpretation to clauses which diverge from this order. I will give some examples from Old English prose. If the neutral order NOUN — ADVERBIALS is disrupted there is almost always an apparent emphasis either on the adverbial or the nouns, e.g.:

> 7 þy ilcan geare gefeaht Æþelhelm dux wiþ Deniscne
> here on Port mid Dornsætum, 7 *gode hwile* þone here
> gefliemde, 7 þa Deniscan ahton wæl stowe gewald (*Chronicle* 837 A.D.)
> 'And the same year General Ethelhelm fought against the Danish army at Port with the men of Dorset, and for a long time held off the Danes, but the Danes won the field'

The adverse outcome of the battle automatically puts the focus on Ethelhelm's temporary success, so that the adverbial *gode hwile* is placed before the direct object.

> Her oþ iewde read Cristes mæl on hefenum æfter sunnan
> setl gonge (*Chronicle* 773 A.D.)
> 'In this year a red cross of Christ appeared in the heavens after sunset'

The startling effect of the sign in the sky has precedence over the verb (which is in second position) and the adverbials of time and place (which are in the normal,

---

[31] Cf. Winfred P. Lehmann, "Some Phonological Observations Based on Examination of the Germanic Consonant Shift", *Monatshefte* 55 (1963) 4:230-31.

neutral position). The noun is focused by having particle and verb in proclisis to it. In the following sentence, also describing a natural (?) phenomenon, the focus is on the verb, which is placed before the less important adverbs, but does not precede the noun (which would have thrown the emphasis on to the noun, as in the preceding example):

> her mona aþistrode on middes wintres mæsse niht (*Chronicle* 827 A.D.)
> 'in this year the moon was eclipsed on the night of Midwinter Mass'

The order ADVERB — OBJECT in the following clause:

> 7 þy geare Ceadwalla *eft* Cent forhergeade (*Chronicle* 687 A.D.)
> 'and the same year Ceadwall again devastated Kent'

is justified by the preceding entry

> Her Ceadwalla 7 Mul Cent 7 Wieht forhergedon (*Chronicle* 686 A.D.)
> 'In this year Ceadwall and Mul devastated Kent and the Isle of Wight'

The lack of an expressive word order in the following clause (which has no surrounding context) makes it impossible to tell which, if any, of the facts presented is in focus:

> Her hæþne men ærest on Sceapige ofer winter sætun (*Chronicle* 855 A.D.)
> 'In this year heathen men for the first time remained throughout the winter on the Isle of Sheppey' [i.e., not Christian men? not subsequent occasions? not on Wight? etc.]

On the basis of a fundamental word-order type we may classify stylistic changes in a text and perhaps better understand the intention of the author. At least theoretically, a study of underlying syntactic patterns may have applications for the study of early literature.

In this study of Germanic syntax I have attempted to describe basic word-order or surface constituent patterns in early Germanic dialects and make observations concerning the sentence structure of Proto-Germanic. Among other things, I have been concerned to show that a basic ordering of SUBJECT — OBJECT — VERB should be reconstructed for Proto-Germanic on the basis of the earliest recorded materials and that this ordering is supported by typological arguments.

This is not the place to describe later developments of word order in Germanic, nor to conjecture about the reasons for the very fundamental changes which have taken place. It is surely significant that the *SOV* word order was retained the longest in English, an isolated and peripheral dialect, and that the shift in the direction of *SVO* ordering increases suddenly in momentum toward the end of the millenium, the period of consolidation of the Norse incursions, and especially after the Conquest. If the hypothesis that Proto-Germanic was a language of the *SOV* type is accepted, it is clear that a general trend was taking place at a very early time toward the *SVO* type, and that this trend affected the Nordic dialects and Gothic first. Most Germanists accept the closer relationship of these two groups in any case. We must assume that already in Proto-Germanic, and probably even in pre-Germanic, the typological characteristics of the language-group were changing.

This change was manifested in several different ways, and had side-effects also·
In addition to the increasing flexibility in the placing of the finite verb, we find especially
in the 'Northern Germanic' group (Gothic, Norse, older Runic incsriptions) alternative positions of the adjective and genitive with respect to the noun developing.
Prepositions replace postpositions at an early stage, although the original situation is
found in certain preverb syntagms (type: *him mid feohtun*) and in the postpositions of
Old Norse poetry. Suffixing is retained as the principal form of affixing, and remains
the sole form of inflection, but the preverbal particles come to be prefixed to the verb
stem (univerbation). In Gothic, however, they are still separate words (*ga-* ⟨ **kom*
shows word-final loss of nasal; enclitics are added to it, e.g., *ga-uh-þan-*). As the languages of the family move toward a more rigid *SVO* ordering, suffixes become
redundant and are eventually lost, or at least greatly reduced.

The reasons for syntactic changes of this kind are not clear. Bach, in an article on
word-order in Amharic,[32] argues that in that language surface *SOV* characteristics
are a superficial and perhaps recent layer, an areal feature acquired from neighbouring
Cushitic languages, and a similar cause may be at work in Indo-European. In Old
Persian the order of constituents was basically *SOV*, and this order is retained until
the time of Arabic influence. At this period the word-order becomes 'free'. In the
modern language, apparently, Persian has the symptoms of a Type I (*VSO*) or Type II
(*SVO*) language, but continues to place the verb at the end.[33] The fact that no specific
group of languages can be pointed to as the cause of the presumed typological
change in Germanic is of less importance than the probable existence of such a cause;
there is no need to assume a mysterious uni-directional 'drift' from one language
type to another.

---

[32] Bach, "Amharic".
[33] Gilbert Lazard, *La langue des plus anciens monuments de la prose persane* (Paris, Klincksieck,
1963), pp. 464-65.

BIBLIOGRAPHY

For information on where the primary sources may be found, see pp. 23-24.

ABBREVIATIONS

IF: *Indogermanische Forschungen*
KZ: *Zeitschrift für Vergleichende Sprachforschung*
BSL: *Bulletin de la Société de Linguistique de Paris*
ZfdA: *Zeitschrift für deutsches Altertum*
JEGP: *Journal of English and Germanic Philology*
AfdA: *Anzeiger für deutsches Altertum*
PBB: *Beiträge zur Geschichte der deutschen Sprache*
TPhS: *Transactions of the Philological Society*
WuS: *Wörter und Sachen*
ZfdPh: *Zeitschrift für deutsche Philologie*
MSL: *Mélanges de la Société de Linguistique de Paris*
Idg.Jb.: *Indogermanisches Jahrbuch*

Åkerlund, Walter, "Fornnordiska ordföljdsprinciper I, II", *Arkiv for Nordisk Filologi* 51 (1935):
    (3.F.): 121-68; 205-51.
——, "Om det finita Verbets Plats i den fornsvenska Bisatsen", *Arkiv for Nordisk Filologi* 57 (1943):
    1-67.
Andrew, S. O., *Syntax and Style in Old English* (Cambridge, Cambridge University Press, 1940).
Aufrecht, Theodor, *Die Hymen des Rigveda*, 3. Auflage (Wiesbaden, Harrassowitz, 1955).
Bach, Emmon, "Is Amharic a SOV language?", *Journal of Ethiopian Languages*, 1970.
Bacquet, Paul, *La structure de la phrase verbale à l'époque alfrédienne* (= *Publications de la Faculté
    des Lettres de l'Université de Strasbourg*, fasc. 145.) (Paris, Les Belles Lettres, 1962).
Behaghel, Otto, "Beziehungen zwischen Umfang und Reihenfolge von Satzgliedern", *IF* 25 (1909):
    110-42.
——, *Deutsche Syntax, eine geschichtliche Darstellung*, 4 vols. (= *Germanische Bibliothek, hrsg.
    von Wilhelm Streitberg. I. Sammlung germanischer Elementar- und Handbücher. 1. Reihe:
    Grammatiken*, 10. Bd.) (Heidelberg, Winter, 1923-32).
——, "Zur Stellung des Verbs im Germanischen und Indogermanischen", *KZ* 56 (1929):276-81.
Behaghel, O., ed., *Heliand und Genesis*, 8. Auflage, bearbeitet von Walther Mitzka (= *Altdeutsche
    Textbibliothek*, Nr. 4) (Tübingen, Niemeyer, 1965).
Bennett, William H., "The Accentuation of Gothic *ga-*" in *Germanic Studies in Honor of Edward
    Henry Sehrt*, Frithjof A. Raven, Wolfram K. Legner, and James Cecil King, eds. (Coral Gables,
    University of Miami Press, 1968) 53-60.
Benveniste, Emile, "La phrase relative: problème de syntaxe générale", *BSL* 53 (1958):39-54.

Bergaigne, A., "Essai sur la construction grammaticale", *Mémoires de la Société de Linguistique* 3 (1869):8-186.

Biener, Claus, "Wie ist die neuhochdeutsche Regel über die Stellung des Verbums entstanden?", *ZfdA* 59 (1921-22):165-78.

——, "Zur Methode der Untersuchungen über die deutsche Wortstellung", *ZfdA* 59 (1921-22): 127-44.

Bloomfield, Leonard, *Language* (Chicago, Holt, 1933).

Bloomfield, Maurice, "On the Variable Position of the Verb in the Oldest Sanskrit", *IF* 31 (1912-13): 156-77.

Botton, W. F., ed., *An Old English Anthology* (Evanston, Ill., Norwestern University Press, 1966).

Bonfante, Giuliano, "Proposizione principale e proposizione dipendente in indoeuropeo", *Archivio Glottologico Italiano* 24 (1930).2:1-60.

de Boor, Helmut, *Studien zur altschwedischen Syntax in den ältesten Gesetztexten und Urkunden.* (= *Germanistische Abhandlungen*, 55 Hft.) (Breslau, Marcus, 1922).

Braune, Wilhelm, "Zur Lehre von der deutschen Wortstellung" in *Forschungen zur deutschen Philologie: Festschrift für R. Hildebrand* (Leipzig, 1894) pp. 34-51.

Braune, Wilhelm, ed., *Althochdeutsches Lesebuch. Zusammengestellt und mit Wörterbuch versehen*, 15. Auflage, bearbeitet von Ernst A. Ebbinghaus (Tübingen, Niemeyer, 1969).

Brooks, Kenneth R., *Andreas and the Fates of the Apostles* (Oxford, Clarendon Press, 1961).

Brugmann, Karl, *Kurze vergleichende Grammatik der indogermanischen Sprachen. Auf Grund des fünfbändigen "Grundrisses der vergleichenden Grammatik der indo-germanischen Sprachen von K. Brugmann und B. Delbrück" verfasst* (Berlin and Leipzig, de Gruyter, 1902-04).

——, *Die Syntax des einfachen Satzes im Indogermanischen* (Berlin, de Gruyter, 1925).

Carlton, Charles, "Word-Order of Modifiers in Old English Prose", *JEGP* 62 (1963).4:778-83.

Curme, George O., *Syntax* (= *A Grammar of the English Language*, vol. III). (Boston, Heath, 1931).

Chomsky, Noam, *Aspects of the Theory of Syntax* (Cambridge, M.I.T. Press, 1965).

Dahlstedt, A., *Rhythm and Word-Order in Anglo-Saxon and Semi-Saxon with Special Reference to Their Development in Modern English* (Lund, Möller, 1901).

Delbrück, Berthold, *Altindische Syntax* (Halle a.S., Buchhandlung des Waisenhauses, 1888).

——, *Germanische Syntax I: Zu den negativen Sätzen* (= *Abh. d. Kgl. Sächs. Akad. d. Wiss., philol.-hist. Kl.*, Bd. 28, No. 4) (Leipzig, Teubner, 1910).

——, *Germanische Syntax II: Zur Stellung des Verbums* (= *Abh. d. Kgl. Sächs. Akad. d. Wiss., philol.-hist. Kl.*, Bd. 28, No. 8) (Leipzig, Teubner, 1911).

——, *Germanische Syntax III: Der altisländische Artikel* (= *Abh. d. Kgl. Sächs. Akad. d. Wiss., philol.-hist. Kl.*, Bd. 33, No. 1) (Leipzig, Teubner, 1916).

——, *Germanische Syntax IV: Die Wortstellung in dem älteren westgötischen Landrecht* (= *Abh. d. Kgl. Sächs. Akad. d. Wiss., philol.-hist. Kl.*, Bd. 36, No. 1) (Leipzig, Teubner, 1918).

——, Review of John Ries, *Die Wortstellung im Beowulf*, *AfdA* 31 (1907):65-76.

——, *Vergleichende Syntax der indogermanischen Sprachen*, 3 vols. Strassburg, Trübner, 1893-1900)

——, "Zur Stellung des Verbums im Gotischen und Altindischen", *PBB* 36 (1910):359-62.

Delbrück, Berthold, and E. Windisch, *Syntaktische Forschungen* (Halle a.S., Buchhandlung des Waisenhauses, 1871).

Diels, P., *Die Stellung des Verbums in der älteren althochdeutschen Prosa* (= *Palaestra No. 59*) (Berlin, Mayer and Müller, 1906).

Dillon, Myles, "Celtic and the Other Indo-European Languages", *TPhS* 1947:15-24.

——, "On the Syntax of the Old Irish Verb", *TPhS* 1955:104-14.

Dover, K. J., *Greek Word Order* (Cambridge, Cambridge University Press, 1960), 72 p.

Erdmann, Oskar, *Grundzüge der deutschen Syntax nach ihrer geschichtlichen Entwicklung*, Erste Abteilung (Stuttgart, Cotta, 1886).

——, Review of John Ries, *Stellung von Subject und Prädikatsverbum im Heliand*, *AfdA* 7 (1881): 191-95.

Ermann, Konrad B., "Beziehungen zwischen Stellung und Funktion der Nebensätze mehrfacher Unterordnung im Althochdeutschen", *ZfdPh* 45 (1913):11-46; 153-216; 426-84.

Falk, Hjalmar and Alf Torp, *Dansk-Norskens syntax i historisk fremstelling* (Kristiana, Aschehoug & Co., 1900).

Fischer, P., "Zur Stellung des Verbums im Griechischen", *Glotta* 13 (1924):1-9; 189-204.

Fourquet, Jean, *L'ordre des éléments de la phrase en germanique ancien. Etudes de syntaxe de position* Strasbourg, 1938. (= *Publications de la Faculté des Lettres de Strasbourg, fasc.* 86) (Strasbourg, 1938).

Friedrich, Johannes, *Hethitisches Elementarbuch*, 2nd ed. (= *Indogermanische Bibliothek. Neue Folge.* 1 *Reihe, Lehr- und Handbücher*) (Heidelberg, Winter, 1960).

Gonda, Jan, *Four Studies in the Language of the Veda* (= *Disputationes Rheno-Trajectinae*, 3) (s'Gravenhage, Mouton, 1959).

——, *Remarques sur la place du verbe dans la phrase active et moyenne en langue sanscrite* (Utrecht, A. Oosthoek, 1953).

Gordon, E. V., *An Introduction to Old Norse*, 2nd ed., revised by A. R. Taylor (Oxford, Clarendon Press, 1957).

Greenberg, Joseph, ed., *Universals of Language*, 2nd ed. (Cambridge, M.I.T. Press, 1966).

Grimm, Jacob, *Deutsche Grammatik*, 4. *Theil: Syntax. Neuer, vermehrter Abdruck, besorgt durch Gustav Roethe und Edward Schroeder* (Gütersloh, Bertelsmann, 1898).

Hermann, E., "Gab es im Indogermanischen Nebensätze?", *KZ* 33 (1894):481-534.

Heusler, Andreas, *Altisländisches Elementarbuch*, 4th ed. (= *Germanische Bibliothek. I. Sammlung germanischer Elementar- und Handbücher. I. Reihe: Grammatiken.* 3. *Bd.*) (Heidelberg, Winter, 1950).

Hirt, Hermann, *Handbuch des Urgermanischen*, 3 vols. (= *Indogermanische Bibliothek.* 1. *Abt.: Sammlung indogermanischer Lehr- und Handbücher.* 1 *Reihe: Grammatiken.* 21 *Bd.*) (Heidelberg, Winter, 1931-32).

——, *Indogermanische Grammatik, V-VII Teile* (Heidelberg, Winter, 1929-36).

Hofmann, J. B., *Lateinische Syntax und Stylistik.* Neubearbeitet von Anton Szantyr (München, Beck, 1965).

Hopper, Paul J., "An Indo-European 'Syntagm' in Germanic", *Linguistics* 54 (1969):39-43.

Hübener, G., "Zur Erklärung der Wortstellungsentwicklung im Angelsächsischen", *Anglia* 39 (1916):277-302.

Jespersen, Otto, *A Modern English Grammar on Historical Principles* (London, Allen & Unwin, 1928).

Kelle, Johann, ed., *Otfrids von Weissenburg Evangelienbuch. Text, Einleitung, Grammatik, Metrik, Glossar*, 3 vols. (Aalen, Zeller, 1963).

Kieckers, Ernst, *Die Stellung des Verbums in Griechischen und in den verwandten Sprachen* (= *Habilitationsschrift — Freiburg i.Br.*) (Strassburg, Trübner, 1911).

——, "Die Stellung der Verba des Sagens in Schaltesätzen im Griechischen und in den verwandten Sprachen", *IF* 30 (1912):145-85.

Kiparsky, Paul, "Tense and Mood in Indo-European Syntax", *Foundations of Language* 4 (1968).1: 30-57.

Klaeber, Friedrich, ed., *Beowulf, and The Fight at Finnsburg, Edited, with Introduction, Bibliography, Notes, Glossary and Appendices*, 3rd ed. with 1st and 2nd supplements (Boston, Heath, 1950).

Kluge, Friedrich, *Urgermanisch. Vorgeschichte der altgermanischen Dialekte*, 3rd ed. (Strassburg, Trübner, 1913).

——, "Zur altgermanischen Sprachgeschichte", *KZ* 26 (1883):68-102, 328.

Koppitz, A., "Gotische Wortstellung", *ZfdPh* 32 (1900):433-63; 33 (1901):7-44.

Krause, Wolfgang, *Handbuch des Gotischen* (= *Handbücher für das germanistische Studium*) (München, Beck, 1953).

——, "Die Wortstellung in den zweigliedrigen Wortverbindungen, untersucht für das Altindische, Litauische und Altnordische", *KZ* 50 (1922):74-128.

Krause, Wolfgang, and Herbert Jankuhn, *Die Runeninschriften im älteren Futhark I: Text* (= *Abh. d. Akad. d. Wiss. in Göttingen. Philol.-hist. Kl.* 3. *Folge, Nr.* 65.) (Göttingen, Vanderhoeck and Ruprecht, 1966).

Kroll, W. "Anfangsstellung des Verbums im Lateinischen", *Glotta* 9 (1918):112-22.

——, "Die Stellung von *esse*" in *Satura Viadrina altera. Festschrift des Philologischen Vereins* (Breslau, 1921) pp. 31-40.

Kuhn, Hans, "Zur Wortstellung und -betonung im Altgermanischen", *PBB* 57 (1933):1-109.

Lakoff, Robin, *Abstract Syntax and Latin Complementation* (= *M.I.T. Research Monograph* No. 49) (Cambridge, MIT Press, 1968).

Laroche, E., "Comparaison du louvite et du lycien", *BSL* 53 (1958):159-97.

Larsson, C., *Ordföljdstudier över det finita verbet i de nordiska fornspraken* (Uppsala Universitets Årsskrift, 1931).

Lazard, Gilbert, *La langue des plus anciens monuments de la prose persane* (= *Etudes Linguistiques* 2) (Paris, Klincksieck, 1963).

Lehmann, Winfred P., *The Alliteration of Old Saxon Poetry* (= *Norsk Tidsskrift for Sprogvidenskap Suppl. bind III* (Oslo, Aschehoug, 1953).

——, "Metrical Evidence for Old English Suprasegmentals", *University of Texas Studies in Literature and Language* I (1959):66-72.

——, "Some Phonological Observations Based on Examination of the Germanic Consonant Shift", *Monatshefte* 55,4 (= *Heffner Festschrift*) (1963):229-35.

——, "The Nordic Languages: Lasting Linguistic Contributions of the Past" in *The Nordic Languages and Modern Linguistics*, Hreinn Benediktsson, ed., (= *Proceedings of the International Conference of Nordic and General Linguistics*) (Reykjavik, Visindafelag Islendinga, 1970) pp. 285-305.

——, "On the Rise of SOV Patterns in New High German", in *Grammatik Kybernetik Kommunikation. Festschrift für Albert Hoppe*, K. G. Schweisthal, ed. (Bonn, Dümmler, 1971) pp. 19-24.

Lenk, Rudolf, "Die Syntax des Skeireins", *PBB* 36 (1910):237-306.

Lindblad, G., *Relativ satsfögning i de nordiska fornspråken* (= *Lunda studier i nordisk språkvetenskap I*) (Lund, Gleerup, 1943).

Löfstedt, Einar, *Syntactica: Studien und Beiträge zur Historischen Syntax des Lateins. Erster Teil: Ueber einige Grundfragen der Lateinischen Nominalsyntax*. Zweite, erweiterte Auflage (=*Skrifter utgivna av Kungl. Humanistiska Vetenskapssamfundet i Lund, X:* 1) (Lund, Gleerup, 1942).

Löhner, R., "Wortstellung der Relativ- und abhängigen Conjunctionalsätze in Notker, *Boethius*", *ZfdPh* 14 (1882):173-217; 300-30.

McCawley, J., "English as a VSO Language", *Language* 46 (1970).2 (Part I):286-99.

McKnight, H., "The Primitive Teutonic Order of Words", *JEGP* 1 (1897):136-219.

Marouzeau, J., *L'ordre des mots en latin* (= *Volume complémentaire: Collection d'Etudes Latines, Série pédagogique* 6) (Paris, Les Belles Lettres, 1953).

Maurer, Friedrich, *Untersuchungen über die deutsche Verbstellung in ihrer geschichtlichen Entwicklung* (= *Germanische Bibliothek. 2. Abt.: Untersuchungen und Texte. 21. Bd.*) (Heidelberg, Winter, 1926).

——, "Zur Bibliographie der indogermanischen Wortstellung", *WuS* 9 (1924):195.

Meillet, Antoine, *Introduction à l'étude comparative des langues indoeuropéennes*, 8th ed. (Paris, Hachette, 1937).

——, "Notes sur quelques faits gothiques", *MSL* 15 (1908-09):73-103.

Minard, A., *La subordination dans la prose védique* (= *Etudes sur la* Śatapathabrāhmana I) (Paris, Les Belles Lettres, 1936).

Mourek, V. E., *Zur Negation im Altgermanischen* (Prague, Verlag der kgl. böhmischen Gesellschaft der Wissenschaften, 1903).

——, "Germanische Syntax", *Acta Philologica Scandinavica* 1 (1926):1-23.

Neckel, Gustav, *Über die altgermanischen Relativsätze* (= *Palaestra No.* 5) (Berlin, Mayer and Müller, 1900).

——, "Vergleichende Syntax auf germanischem Gebiet", *Verhandlungen der Idg. Sektion auf der 54. Versammlung deutscher Philologen und Schulmänner in Münster*, 1923. (Summary in *Idg. Jb.* 9 (1922-23):290-91).

Neckel, Gustav, ed. *Edda. Die Lieder des Codex Regius nebst verwandten Denkmälern. I. Text.* 3., umgearbeitete Auflage von Hans Kuhn (= *Germanische Bibliothek. 4. Reihe: Texte*) (Heidelberg, Winter, 1962).

Nygaard, M., *Norrøn Syntax* (Kristiana, Aschehoug & Co., 1905).

——, "Verbets stilling i sætningen i det norrøne sprog", *Arkiv for Nordisk Filologi* 12 (1900):209-40.

Paul, Hermann, *Deutsche Grammatik Bd. III, T.* 4 (2. *Hälfte*): *Syntax* (Halle a S., Niemeyer, 1919).

Plummer, Charles, *Two of the Saxon Chronicles, Parallel... Edited, with Introduction, Notes, Appendices and Glossary on the Basis of an Edition by John Earle, M. A.*, 2 vols. (Oxford, Clarendon Press, 1965).

Prokosch, E., *A Comparative Germanic Grammar* (Philadelphia, University of Pennsylvania, 1939). (Linguistic Society of America).

Rieger, Max, "Die alt- und angelsächsische Verskunst", *ZfdPh* 7 (1876):1-63.

Ries, H., "Über althochdeutsche Wortfolge", *ZfdPh* 33 (1901):212-38; 230-349.

Ries, John, "Zur altsächsischen Genesis: II: Zur Wortstellung", *ZfdA* 40 (1896):270-89.

——, Review of W. Ruhfus *Die Stellung des Verbums im althochdeutschen Tatian*, *AfdA* 25 (1899), 16-21.

——, *Die Stellung von Subject und Prädicatsverbum im Heliand. Nebst einem Anhang metrischer Excurse. Ein Beitrag zur germanischen Wortstellungslehre* (= *Quellen und Forschungen zur Sprach- und Kulturgeschichte der germanischen Völker*, 41) (Strassburg, Trübner, 1880).

——, *Die Wortstellung im Beowulf* (Halle, Niemeyer, 1907).

Rosenkranz, B., "Die Stellung des attributiven Genetivs im Italischen", *IF* 51 (1933):131-39.

Ross, J. R., "Gapping and the Order of Constituents" in *Progress in Linguistics*, M. Bierswisch and K. E. Heidolph, eds. (The Hague, Mouton, 1970) pp. 249-259.

Roth, W. "Die Wortstellung im Aussagehauptsatz angelsächsischer Originalprosa", Diss.-Berlin (Berlin, 1914).

Rothstein, Ewald, *Die Wortstellung in der Peterborough Chronik mit bes. Berücksichtigung des dritten Teiles gegenüber den beiden ersten in Bezug auf den Sprachübergang von der Synthese zur Analyse* (= *Studien zur englischen Philologie, Heft* 64) (Diss.-Halle, 1915) (Halle a.S., Niemeyer, 1922).

Rübens, G., *Parataxe und Hypotaxe in dem ältesten Teil der Sachsenchronik* (*Parker HS bis zum Jahre* 891), (= Studien zur englischen *Philologie, Heft*. 56) (Halle a.S., Niemeyer, 1915).

Schneider, Karl, *Die Stellungstypen des finiten Verbs im urgermanischen Haupt- und Nebensatz* (= *Untersuchungen und Texte* 41) (Heidelberg, Winter, 1938).

Scholten, W. E., "Satzverbindende Partikeln bei Tatian und Otfrid", *PBB* 22 (1897):391-423.

Schuchart, Richard, *Die Negation im Beowulf* (= *Berliner Beiträge zur germanischen und romanischen Philologie* 38, *germanische Abt. no.* 25) (Berlin, Ebering, 1910).

Schulze, Wilhelm, "Personalpronomen und Subjektsausdruck im Gotischen", in *Beiträge zur germanischen Sprachwissenschaft: Festschrift für Otto Behaghel* (Heidelberg, Winter, 1924) pp. 92-109.

Schwentner, Ernst, "Bibliographie zur idg. Wortstellung 1823-1923", *WuS* 8 (1923):179; 9 (1924): 194.

——, *Die primären Interjektionen der indogermanischen Sprachen* (= *Indogermanische Bibliothek. III. Abt.: Untersuchungen*, 5) (Heidelberg, Winter, 1924).

Shannon, Ann, *A Descriptive syntax of the Parker manuscript of the Anglo-Saxon Chronicle from 734 to 891* (= *Janua Linguarum; Studia Memoriae Nicolai van Wijk Dedicata. Series Practica*, 14) (The Hague, Mouton, 1964).

Streitberg, Wilhelm, *Urgermanische Grammatik*, 3rd ed. (= *Germanische Bibliothek, I. Abt., Elementar- und Handbücher. I. Reihe, Grammatiken* 1.) (Heidelberg, Winter, 1963).

Streitberg, Wilhelm, ed., *Die Gotische Bibel*, 5th ed. (Heidelberg, Winter, 1965).

Sturtevant, Edgar, *A Comparative Grammar of the Hittite Language*, 2nd ed., revised, vol. 1 with Adelaide E. Hahn (= *William Dwight Whitney Linguistic Series*) (New Haven, Yale University Press, 1951-0000).

Surtevant, Edgar, and George Bechtel, *A Hittite Chrestomathy* (= *William Dwight Whitney Linguistic Series*) (Philadelphia, Linguistic Society of America, 1935).

Sweet, Henry, *A New English Grammar, Logical and Historical. Part II: Syntax* (= *Oxford Press Series*), 2 vols. (Oxford, Clarendon Press, 1892-98).

Thurneysen, Rudolf, *A Grammar of Old Irish, Revised and Enlarged Edition, Translated from the German by D. A. Binchy and Osborn Bergin* (Dublin, Institute for Advanced Studies, 1961).

Todt, August, "Die Wortstellung im Beowulf", *Anglia* 16 (1894):226-60.

Tomanetz, K., Review of Ries, *Stellung von Subject und Prädicatsverbum im Heliand*, *Deutsche Literaturzeitung* II (1881).8:275-76.

——, *Die Relativsätze bei den althochdeutschen Übersetzern des 8. und 9. Jahrhunderts* (Wien, Geroldssohn, 1879).

Twaddell, W. F., "A Main Clause with 'final' verb in Notker's *Boethius*", *JEGP* 31 (1932):403-06.

Vachek, Joseph, *The Linguistic School of Prague: An Introduction to its Theory and Practice.* (= *Indiana University Studies in the History and Theory of Linguistics*) (Bloomington, Indiana University Press, 1966).

Vendryes, J. "La place du verbe en celtique", *Mélanges de la Société de Linguistique* 17 (1912): 337-51.

Wackernagel, Jacob, "Über ein Gesetz der indogermanischen Wortstellung", *IF* 1 (1892):333-435.

——, *Vorlesungen über Syntax, mit besonderer Berücksichtigung von Griechisch, Lateinisch und Deutsch*, 2 vols. (Basel, Birkhäuser, 1920).

Watkins, Calvert, "Preliminaries to a Historical and Comparative Analysis of the Syntax of the Old Irish Verb", *Celtica* 6 (1963):1-49.

——, "Preliminaries to the Reconstruction of Indo-European Sentence Structure" in *Proceedings of the Ninth International Congress of Linguists* (The Hague, Mouton, 1964) pp. 1035-45.

Weil, Henri, *De l'ordre des mots dans les langues anciennes comparées aux langues modernes: question de grammaire générale.* 3rd ed. (= *Collection Philologique* 3) (Paris, Vieweg, 1879).

Wenning, Einar A., *Studier över ordföljden i fornsvenskan: I. Predikatets bestämningar i äldre och yngre fornsvenskan* (Lund, Lindstedt, 1930).

Wessén, Elias, ed., *Fornsvenska Texter. Mid Förklaringar och Ordlista*, Andra, utökade Upplagan (= *Nordisk Filologi, Texter och Lärobocker för Universitetsstudier. A. Texter* 10) (Stockholm, Svenska Bökförlaget, 1959).

Whitney, William D., *Sanskrit Grammar*, 2nd ed. (= *Bibliothek indogermanischer Grammatiken, Bd. II*) (Leipzig, Breitkopf & Härtel, 1889).

Wunderlich, Hermann, *Beiträge zur Syntax des Notker'schen Boethius* (Berlin, Schade, 1883). (Diss.-Berlin).

INDEX